The
Groom's
Game Plan

Getting to the Altar and Surviving the Trip

Dan Jewel
Illustrations by Greg Stadler

BARNES
& NOBLE
BOOKS

NEW YORK

A BARNES & NOBLE BOOK

©2005 by Barnes & Noble Publishing, Inc.

Illustrations ©Greg Stadler

Library of Congress Cataloging-in-Publication Data

Jewel, Dan.
    The groom's game plan : getting to the altar and surviving
the trip / by Dan Jewel.
        p. cm.
    ISBN 0-7607-5817-4 (alk. paper)
1. Weddings—Planning. 2. Bridegrooms. I. Title.

    HQ745.J49 2004
    395.2'2—dc22

                                                2004016086

Printed by WKT, Ltd in China

1 3 5 7 9 10 8 6 4 2

Contents

Introduction
5

Chapter One
GETTING ENGAGED
15

Chapter Two
FIRST STEPS
31

Chapter Three
PICKING THE PLAYERS
47

Chapter Four
GETTING BUSY
*Planning Ahead for
Your Wedding Day*
55

Chapter Five
THE CLOTHES MAKE THE
MAN
69

Chapter Six
THE FUN STUFF
The Honeymoon
85

Chapter Seven
THE PRESSURE'S ON
*The Rehearsal Dinner
(and Other Activities)*
103

Chapter Eight
THE NITTY GRITTY
117

Chapter Nine
GIVING AND GETTING
133

Chapter Ten
THE REALLY FUN STUFF
The Bachelor Party
145

Chapter Eleven
THE BIG DAY
155

Conclusion
AFTER THE BIG DAY
167

Index
173

Introduction

So this is it. You've met that perfect someone. You know she's perfect because the notion of spending the rest of your days and nights with her fills you not with horror and revulsion, but with an embarrassingly giddy sensation. You're willing—eager, even—to put your swinging single days behind you.

You've decided to get married. Congratulations.

Now comes the challenging part.

The months leading up to a wedding are filled, naturally, with excitement and joy. However, they also tend to come with a fair share of stress. If you and your partner are like most couples, the majority of the responsibility for planning your wedding—and, hence, the majority of that stress—will fall squarely on your fiancée's shoulders. So a significant part of your job as groom consists of being hugely supportive, constantly offering to help, and remembering that your bride-to-be is under a lot of pressure and prone to homicidal rages (consider it good practice for pregnancy). Remember: You don't want to give her reasons to start thinking, "My God, why did I agree to marry this insensitive lout?"

If you've already got the supportive, sensitive-guy act down, don't think you can just relax and tell yourself what a great groom you are. There are many specific wedding planning tasks for which you, the male half of the couple, are responsible. That's what this book is about. It spells out the things you need to know and the steps you need to take so that you can stay on track without your fiancée having to nag you.

Above all, as you plan your wedding, try not to let the pressure take over, and don't get so bogged down in details that you lose sight of the bigger picture. Stop every now and then, take a deep breath, and remind yourself of what's waiting for you at the end: a beautiful bride, a lifetime of happiness together, and lots and lots of dinners with the in-laws.

Uh...So What Do I Have to Do?

Traditionally speaking, the division of wedding planning duties works out pretty much as outlined below.

The Groom

* Plan the rehearsal dinner (traditionally hosted by the groom's parents)
* Arrange for wedding day attire—for yourself and the groomsmen
* Make arrangements to obtain the marriage license
* Plan the honeymoon
* Shop, with the bride, for wedding bands
* Attend a bachelor party
* Purchase tokens of appreciation for the groomsmen
* Get dressed and show up on time on the wedding day

The Bride

* Everything else, including possibly suffering a nervous breakdown

Notice that the word *traditionally* is used to describe this division of labor. In the modern era, you, the groom, are expected to share the planning with your bride. A wedding is a massive amount of work, and if you attempt to do only the bare minimum, you may not actually make it to the altar.

It seems obvious, but when it comes to divvying up the duties, the most important thing you can do is sit down and talk to your bride. Maybe she's thrilled to deal with most of the details on her own—or with a little help from some of her female friends—and thinks you'd only get in the way. In that case, congratulations: You just won the wedding planning equivalent of the lottery. Or maybe she's hoping that the two of you will plan every step of the wedding together. Do your best to make her happy—without making yourself miserable along the way. It's called compromise, and you'll have to get used to it. It's what marriage is all about.

Timeline: What to Do and When to Do It

If you want to be involved—deeply, disturbingly involved—in planning every single detail of your wedding, here's an overview of the areas you'll need to tackle and a suggested time frame for doing so. For those of you who prefer to take a more hands-off approach, pay attention to the points that appear in italics and gloss over the rest.

✓ Nine Months Before–If Not Sooner

- [ ] *Propose (and convince her to accept), if you haven't done so already*
- [ ] *Set up a time for your parents and hers to meet, both to celebrate your engagement and to chat about your upcoming wedding*
- [ ] *Have a conversation about the budget—with each other and any family members helping out—and settle on a firm figure*
- [ ] *Select a wedding date, along with backup dates in case your ideal site is booked*
- [ ] *Put together the guest list*
- [ ] Hire a wedding consultant, if you think you need one
- [ ] *Book a ceremony site*
- [ ] *Book a reception venue*
- [ ] *Find an officiant to perform the ceremony*

- [ ] *Decide who to have as your best man and groomsmen, and ask whomever you've chosen to participate*
- [ ] Book a caterer
- [ ] Book musicians to play at the ceremony
- [ ] Hire a band/DJ to play at the reception

✓ Six to Nine Months Before

- [ ] Book a photographer
- [ ] Book a videographer
- [ ] Hire a florist
- [ ] Reserve any necessary rental items
- [ ] Map out a menu with the caterer, and arrange for a tasting
- [ ] Order wedding invitations (and, while you're at it, any other needed stationery items, such as thank-you cards and wedding announcements)
- [ ] Send save-the-date cards
- [ ] Arrange to hold blocks of hotel rooms for nonlocal guests
- [ ] *Make arrangements for your wedding night accommodations*
- [ ] *Start researching possible honeymoon spots (for a detailed timeline outlining the specific steps involved in planning the honeymoon, see page 86)*
- [ ] *If you're planning to travel to another country for your wedding or honeymoon, update passports and other travel documents, and find out if any immunizations are required*
- [ ] Hire a calligrapher (to address invitations and announcements, write place cards, etc.)
- [ ] *Register for gifts*

Four to Six Months Before

- ☐ *Make necessary reservations for the honeymoon*
- ☐ Set the time for the ceremony rehearsal
- ☐ *Book a spot for the rehearsal dinner (or decide to have it at your parents' place), and start thinking about the details*
- ☐ *Buy or arrange to rent your wedding day attire*
- ☐ *Make arrangements for groomsmen's attire (you pick, they pay)*
- ☐ Obtain wedding favors, if desired
- ☐ Sit down with the florist to make specific selections
- ☐ *Select or approve boutonnieres for yourself, your groomsmen, and prominent male family members (with your bride's help, of course)*
- ☐ Make arrangements for the wedding cake (and a groom's cake, if desired)
- ☐ *Purchase gifts for your groomsmen*
- ☐ Address invitations (or have someone do so)
- ☐ *Advise your best man of any bachelor party guidelines*

Two to Four Months Before

- ☐ Send information regarding accommodations, transportation, and local points of interest to out-of-towners on the guest list (it's a good idea to do this earlier if the wedding is in a tourist area during peak season)
- ☐ *Research marriage license requirements and deadlines*
- ☐ Arrange for wedding day transportation for yourself, the bride, the wedding party, and immediate family members
- ☐ *Shop for wedding rings, and purchase bride's*
- ☐ *Go over the details of the ceremony with the officiant (along with your bride)*

☐ Choose readings or songs to personalize the ceremony—and ask friends and family who you want to read or sing if they'll do so

☐ *If you're composing your vows, get moving*

☐ Pick music for the ceremony

☐ Decide upon tunes for your first dance, the cake-cutting ceremony, any group dances, and any other reception rituals

☐ *Finalize the arrangements for the rehearsal dinner*

☐ *Get a present for your bride, if you're exchanging gifts*

☐ *Obtain a thank-you gift for your parents (not obligatory, but a nice touch)*

☐ *If your bride will be changing into a going-away outfit for your grand exit from the reception, choose one for yourself that matches the formality of hers*

☐ Mail wedding invitations (six to eight weeks prior to the event)

☐ *Extend invitations for the rehearsal dinner (should happen shortly after the wedding invitations have been sent)*

☐ Look into newspapers' deadlines and guidelines for wedding announcements

☐ *Sit for portrait to be used in newspaper announcement (may include bride and groom or just the bride)*

Four to Six Weeks Before

☐ *Arrange for blood tests (if required by law)*

☐ *Get your marriage license (you may need to do this at a different point in time depending on local regulations; be sure to consult the local town clerk's office well in advance)*

☐ Submit wedding announcement to newspapers (should be done according to each publication's deadline requirements)

☐ Organize/assemble welcome baskets for out-of-towners

☐ Provide DJ/band with a list of songs to be played—and ones you don't want to hear

☐ *If you bought your tux or suit, pick it up—and make sure it fits*

☐ *Pick up the wedding bands from the jeweler*

☐ *Casually ask your best man how his toast is coming along to make sure he hasn't forgotten all about it*

☐ *Enjoy your bachelor party (usually occurs anytime from this point until a couple of days before the wedding)*

☐ *Begin plotting out the seating chart (along with bride)*

Two Weeks Before

☐ Give the reception site manager and/or caterer the final head count (exact timing varies; be sure to meet the deadline specified in each contract)

☐ *Provide the site manager and/or caterer for the rehearsal dinner with the final head count (exact timing varies; be sure to meet the deadline[s] specified by the site and/or caterer)*

☐ Finish the seating plan

☐ Fill out place cards, or have the calligrapher do so

☐ *Prepare a toast to give at the rehearsal dinner and, if you so choose, one for the reception*

☐ Give the photographer and/or videographer a list of requested shots

☐ Put together a complete schedule of the reception events for all service providers who will need it, such as the band/disc jockey, caterer, venue manager, photographer, and videographer

☐ *Make arrangements for someone to take care of your pets, water plants, and/or house-sit while you're away, if applicable*

☐ If you bought new shoes for the wedding, wear them around the house a bit so you don't wind up with blisters

☐ Get a decent haircut

One Week Before

☐ Panic

☐ Relax and remember it's normal to panic

☐ If you're renting your wedding day attire, pick it up—and make sure it fits

☐ Make sure your groomsmen pick up their rented attire

☐ Confirm reservations for your wedding night accommodations

☐ Confirm all reservations for the honeymoon (transportation to and from destination, transportation in and around destination, hotel, etc.)

☐ Get crisp bills for tips for wedding service providers (this only applies to services you're paying for, obviously)

☐ Get final payments ready for service providers who must be paid on the wedding day (again, only for the services you're covering)

☐ Put together a list of everything you need to bring to the rehearsal, rehearsal dinner, and wedding, and gather all of these items together (see the card at the end of this book for guidance regarding what to bring to the wedding site)

☐ Pack—for the wedding and honeymoon

☐ Confirm arrangements with all service providers

☐ Contact the post office to have your mail held while you're away

☐ Stop newspaper delivery

☐ Tell stores where you've registered to hold deliveries while you're away

✓ One Day Before

- ☐ Bring welcome baskets to hotel(s) for nonlocal wedding guests
- ☐ *Attend the ceremony rehearsal*
- ☐ *Make sure groomsmen know exactly what they need to do the next day*
- ☐ *Enjoy the rehearsal dinner*
- ☐ *Give gifts to the members of your wedding party*
- ☐ *Give thank-you gift to your parents (if you've decided to do so)*
- ☐ *Give your bride her gift, if you're exchanging presents*
- ☐ *Try, against all odds, to get a decent night's sleep*

Chapter One

Getting Engaged

Let's start at the very beginning. If you view proposing as just a mandatory step you need to get out of the way before you get married, start rewiring your brain. Women expect two things: a ring and serious romance. (For those of you who have already done the proposal thing, skip ahead to page 27.)

THE REALITY OF RINGS

Get that image out of your head. You know the one—you've seen it in every romantic movie ever made: The guy brings out the ring, the woman is utterly shocked, and both are overjoyed. What the movie doesn't show is what happens next. She gets a closer look and thinks, "Ugh—that's the most hideous ring I've ever seen!" And every day and night for the rest of her life, every time she looks at her ring finger, she's reminded that she married a dolt with no taste (except in women).

So, rule number one of ring shopping: Get the inside scoop. One option is to check out rings with your fiancée-to-be. This doesn't mean you have to drag her along, get her to pick out a ring, and then propose in the store. The next time you're in a jewelry shop, point to something you love and ask her what she thinks. Or point out the most ostentatious piece you can find and see whether she finds it as distasteful as you do. (While you're there, you might want to have her sized for a ring so you don't end up proposing with a piece of jewelry that she'll need to part with temporarily.) If she's got friends or relatives who are engaged or married, ask her what she thinks of their rings. That way you can get some general guidelines—but still surprise her with the specifics.

If you'd prefer to keep the ring and proposal a total surprise—and if you feel that this is what your fiancée-to-be would really want—go shopping with one of her sisters or one of her close female friends (anyone near and dear to her who possesses two X chromosomes). To get the size right, borrow one of her other rings and have the jeweler measure. Just don't let her catch you raiding her jewelry box.

Rule number two: When you finally own the engagement ring, get it insured. Fast.

Romantic and Ring-Free

One surefire way to avoid buying the wrong ring is to propose without one, then go ring shopping with your fiancée. This has its risks; for some women, a proposal just isn't a proposal without a diamond ring to seal the deal. Still, even a ringless proposal can be romantic if you offer her a substitute—an elegant necklace or a pair of earrings, or even an extravagant bouquet of flowers—and tell her that you've scheduled an appointment to meet with a jeweler together on the coming weekend. A word of warning: Do not present a piece of wire or the sort of ring that comes free in a Cracker Jack box. That's only cute if you're four years old and it's a pretend marriage.

THE FOUR CS

The traditional engagement ring consists of a solitaire diamond (a single stone) and a platinum, white gold, or gold band. Before you hand over your life savings for a diamond, you should know the basics. They're called the four Cs, and they determine the quality and value of the gem. Because you're probably not a jeweler—and if you are, why are you reading this section?—you won't be able to judge these elements for yourself. Regardless of where you buy the ring—whether at an upscale store or in the diamond district—don't just accept what the jeweler is telling you; he/she should give you a certificate from the Gemological Institute of America (GIA), which rates the diamonds in each of these categories. Here's the 411 on the four Cs.

1. Clarity: The easiest way to get snookered by a shady diamond dealer is on clarity. Nearly all diamonds have flaws, known as inclusions (tiny fractures, clouds of minerals, or air bubbles inside the diamond) and blemishes (scratches or nicks on the stone's surface), that are completely invisible to the naked eye but can significantly lower the value of the jewel. The GIA ranks clarity as follows:

FL (Flawless): The finest diamonds reveal no inclusions or blemishes, even under 10x magnification. This type of diamond is exceedingly rare and staggeringly expensive.

IF (Internally Flawless): These stones still show no inclusions under magnification, but have some very minor blemishes. Diamonds with this rating are also extremely rare and expensive.

VVS1 and VVS2 (Very Very Slightly Included): These stones contain inclusions that are extremely difficult for experts to spot under magnification. In this category, as in the ones below, a lower number means higher quality.

VS1 and VS2 (Very Slightly Included): Small crystal formations or clouds are visible under magnification, but still take some effort to spot.

SI1 and SI2 (Slightly Included): Inclusions are easily visible to an expert under 10x magnification.

I1 to I3 (Included): The most flawed stones have clouds or cracks visible to the naked eye. Even if you're trying to cut costs, you should not purchase a diamond with an I rating.

2. Color: The finest, most expensive stones are colorless. The less color, the higher the value of the diamond. The GIA rates color from best to worst as follows.

* D to F (colorless)

* G to J (near colorless)

* K to M (faint yellow)

* N to R (very light yellow)

* S to Z (light yellow)

Generally, anything between D and J looks colorless to the naked eye. On the lower end, you'll see clear hints of yellow, brown, or gray. Sounds simple, right? Well, here's the confusing part: There's another category of vibrantly colored stones—pink, blue, green, yellow, or brown diamonds—known as "fancy colored diamonds," which are actually far more costly than colorless diamonds (think the Hope Diamond, which, just in case you're wondering, is out of your price range). They're rated by the GIA on a separate nine-point scale, from "faint" to the rarest "fancy vivid" colored stones. For more on colored diamonds, consult the GIA website at www.gia.org.

3. Cut: Technically, this refers to the way the diamond is cut (hence the term), but it's more commonly used to define the shape of the diamond. The reason you care? The cut determines how light reflects off the surface—and, hence, how much the diamond sparkles. A poorly cut diamond will sit there like a lump of glass. A well-cut one will shine and win your fiancée loads of attention. The most common cuts include:

Round/brilliant: This round-shaped stone offers blinding sparkle. If you want a diamond that will garner stares from across a crowded room, brilliant is your best bet.

Emerald: This classic favorite is rectangular in shape.

Princess: Shaped like a square, this cut is dressed up with a fancier name.

Pear: The stone resembles a teardrop in shape.

Oval: It's shaped like an oval (go figure), rounded at both ends.

Marquise: The stone is cut like an oval, but pointed at both ends.

 Heart-shaped: You guessed it—this one looks like a heart.

If that's not overwhelming enough, high-end stores such as Tiffany and Cartier have created their own custom cuts. The GIA has no formal grading system for cut, but it rates two important components—polish (the quality of the surface of each facet in a diamond) and symmetry (which takes into account any misalignments or off-center appearances)—as excellent, very good, good, fair, or poor.

4. Carat: Carat refers to the weight of the diamond. Some women will prefer a smaller stone of exquisite quality, while others just want people to say, "Look at the size of that rock!" Though bigger sounds better, a huge diamond may look absurd on a tiny hand—another reason to consider bringing your potential bride to try on rings.

THE SETTING

At many jewelry stores, you'll be looking at diamonds that are already set in rings; at others, you're purchasing a loose diamond—which means you still need to pick the actual ring, purchase it, and have the jeweler put the two elements together. Typically, engagement rings are either platinum, gold, or white gold. Platinum is strongest and tends to show off the diamond to best effect. Of course, it's also the most expensive, but once you've paid for the actual diamond, everything else seems cheap. White gold (which looks much like platinum) and yellow gold are less expensive—but also far less durable.

The most common way to attach the stone is with a prong setting, which holds the diamond above the band. This causes the stone to look larger and allows more light to hit it, so it sparkles.

Smart Shopping

While there are many reputable jewelry sources out there, you don't want to find out later on that you've been had. Check any dealer you're considering with the Better Business Bureau, and use places that come highly recommended by friends and family. And don't forget to get a GIA certificate.

The drawbacks? If your fiancée bashes her hand against a wall, a poorly set diamond that isn't secure could pop out. In a flush setting, the stone is embedded in the band, which is best if your potential bride is, say, a mountain climber or a boxer. It's also a more modern look. With either type of setting, you can place smaller diamonds on either side of the main stone to vary the look. Again, it's all a matter of taste—hers, not yours.

MONEY-SAVING TIPS:
BUYING AN ENGAGEMENT RING

Call it the fifth C: cost. There's some vague rule floating around that says guys should spend about two months' salary on an engagement ring. Ignore that rule. You should simply spend as much as you feel comfortable spending. Here are a few points to help you save money and get the biggest bang for your buck—without sacrificing quality.

* Emerald, oval, marquise, and pear cuts look larger than round diamonds of the same exact weight.

* Setting two small diamonds—or other gems—on either side of the main diamond will make that stone look larger. Baguettes, which are small and rectangular, are popular side stones.

* Many jewelry stores have diamond sales after Christmas and Valentine's Day. And summer tends to be a slow season, so prices may be lower than at other times of the year.

* Consider alternatives to diamonds. Rubies, emeralds, sapphires, and other precious stones are popular options, and choosing a ring with your fiancée's birthstone lends a personal touch. But beware: Many seemingly open-minded, ultramodern brides are still ultratraditional when it comes to engagement rings and may be heartbroken if they don't see a diamond. Before you consider this option, get a female friend or relative of hers to ask what she really thinks of diamondless engagement rings.

Questions to Ask: Ring Shopping

* How long will it take before the ring is ready to be picked up?

* If it doesn't fit properly, can we bring it in to resize it? Is there an additional charge to resize the ring? *(If you're surprising her with the ring, the chances of it fitting perfectly are slim to none. A jeweler should be willing to resize the ring at minimal cost.)*

* Does the cost include the ring and the setting? If not, what's the price of the diamond itself? How much does the band cost? And how much does it cost to set the stone?

* How much of a deposit is required?

* When is the balance due?

* What is the return/exchange policy? *(If your spouse-to-be does not like the ring, you should be able to exchange it for another of equal value. Make sure to get the policy in writing.)*

* What are the exact grades this diamond has gotten for cut, clarity, color, and carat?

* Is there an official certificate from the GIA for this diamond? *(Beware of any diamond that doesn't come with a GIA certificate.)*

* *If the stone doesn't come with a GIA certificate, ask if you can get it appraised, and pose the following question:* If the GIA contradicts the ratings you've given me, can I return the diamond? *(If the answer to this question is yes, make sure to get that policy in writing. If the answer is no, turn and walk out the door.)*

A SERIOUS PROPOSITION

You've got the ring. You've had it insured. You're bankrupt. It's time to propose.

Just as you did when you bought the ring, you need to consider your beloved's tastes and style when figuring out how to propose. Before you ask her the big question, ask yourself a few.

Is the type of proposal I'm considering geared toward her likes or mine? If she's a huge Yankees fan, seeing "Will you marry me?" up on the scoreboard during the seventh inning stretch might be perfect. If she thinks baseball is boring and you tend to get drunk and heckle the players, that's probably not how she'd like to be asked. You want the moment to be special for both of you. But more to the point, you want the moment to be special for her.

Is she an exhibitionist or a private person? Even the most simple, traditional method of proposing—getting down on one knee and asking—can vary according to taste. If she's on the shy side, a proposal in a public place such as a restaurant may make her uncomfortable. Proposing during a candlelight dinner at your pad, on the other hand, may be ideal.

Do I need to run this by her parents first? Whether you should ask for permission from her parents (or, traditionally, her father) beforehand is a touchy issue. Hopefully, by the time you get around to asking someone to marry you, you've actually gotten to know her. If she has a traditional, conservative, old-fashioned family, it's worth making that phone call—or, if possible, paying a personal visit. If not, calling her parents immediately after you've become engaged is perfectly appropriate.

ALL IN THE ASKING

If you're creatively challenged, here are some ideas for how to ask the most important question you'll ever ask (until "Honey, is it okay if there are strippers at the bachelor party?").

Literary Love: Compose and recite a love poem that ends with a proposal. Or hand her a cute story you've written about the history of your relationship—and have it conclude with you asking for her hand in marriage.

The Couch Potato: Make a video of yourself down on one knee, popping the question. Invite her over to watch a sappy chick flick. Then pop your cassette in the VCR.

Extreme Measures: Propose atop a mountain, while tandem sky-diving, or under the stars in the middle of a camping trip. Of course, in these situations, you might want to give her the ring when you're back home.

Movie Madness: You know those dull, repetitive ads that play before the lights go down in a movie theater? Talk to the manager

Guru Grooms on...

Bad Proposals

"A friend went on a business trip. When he arrived home, his then-girlfriend was waiting for him. He had very stupidly tied the engagement ring on a ribbon around his...well, use your imagination. He then tried to convince her to get amorous, thinking it would be amusing for her to find the ring that way. She refused— he had just come off a long flight and hadn't bathed. He insisted really hard, and she refused really hard. Eventually, he had to give up and fish out the ring for her."

—*Aun, 31, Singapore*

about getting a slide that asks your girlfriend to marry you. Just don't let her run out for popcorn at the wrong moment.

Web Spinning: Create a website with bells and whistles—photos of the two of you, romantic music, the works—and have the magic question scroll across the screen.

Plane and Simple: Take her on a picnic or spend a day at the beach, and hire a plane to sky-write a proposal—or fly a banner asking for her hand.

Happy Trails: Create a path of flower petals or votive candles leading to the engagement ring.

Treasure Island: Make up a treasure hunt with clues leading her to some meaningful spots in your relationship. Final stop: you—and the ring.

The Oldie but Goodie: For most women, a proposal is a grand gesture in and of itself. Find the right spot—a romantic restaurant, a garden, the site of your first date—and the right moment. Get down on one knee (it's old-fashioned, and women dream of it). Tell her how much you love her, how happy she makes you, and how you want to spend the rest of your life with her. But go the extra mile. If you're in a restaurant, tell the maître d' that it's a very special occasion so that you get a romantic table. If you're doing it in your studio apartment, light some candles, open some champagne, put on Barry White—and pick your dirty socks off the floor.

Indecent Proposals: What NOT to Do

1. You may have met online, but it doesn't matter: E-mail is not romantic. Ever. Don't propose via e-mail or instant message. It's like calling and asking her to marry you over the phone, which, by the way, is another no-no.

2. You're at a fine restaurant. The waiter brings her a glass of champagne, and there, at the bottom, is a diamond engagement ring. Nothing could be more romantic...until she swallows the ring. Or chokes on it. Keep the ring out of beverages.

3. Likewise, putting a ring in some sort of culinary concoction is, at best, a mess. At worst, a stomach pump is in your near future.

4. Asking her parents' permission before proposing is one thing. Proposing in front of her family or friends is another. She may want to cry. She may want to kiss you. She may want to scream with joy. (Most likely she'll try all three at once.) But these are things she won't want to do while her parents are standing there.

MEET THE FOLKS

You proposed. She said yes. Whew. If you haven't done so already, you and the bride will need to introduce your families to one another. Here are a few tips.

* Pick a neutral setting, such as dinner at a casual restaurant. This will put everyone on level footing and remove the pressures that come along with hosting a get-together at someone's home.

* Avoid any place that's too formal, as this can make the people involved even less relaxed. That said, you probably also want to stay away from joints specializing in ribs, lobster, or other messy-to-eat foods that could make some people feel self-conscious.

* If your parents live at opposite ends of the earth, no one has to hop on a plane right away. (Traditionally, the burden falls on the groom's parents to extend themselves, so they should call the bride's family and express congratulations.) That said, it's a very, very good idea to arrange an actual face-to-face meeting before the supremely stressful wedding weekend arrives. Consider a weekend getaway where your families can mix; try to pick a midway point so that no one feels put out.

HOW TO IMPRESS YOUR FUTURE IN-LAWS

1. Pretend you're going to a job interview. Dress well (overdressing a tad is much better than underdressing). Maintain eye contact. Offer a solid handshake. Smile a lot.

2. If you're having dinner at your future in-laws' or spending a weekend there, come bearing gifts (this is a must). A vase or some other decorative item is a safe bet, but let your fiancée guide you. She knows their tastes.

3. Avoid hot-button issues. You can have lighthearted, good-natured debates about movies, sports, restaurants, and the

morality of reality television. You should not, however, discuss politics, religion, or the morality of premarital sex.

4. Gentlemanly gestures are key. Hold open doors for your future in-laws, your parents, and your fiancée. Help your fiancée with her coat. When any of the women get up from the table, do that quaint half-stand thing. You'll look old-fashioned, and parents love that stuff.

5. Display impeccable table manners. Place your napkin on your lap, and chew with your mouth closed. Don't talk with your mouth full, don't slurp your soup or beverage, and don't snap your fingers or call out "Garçon" in order to get the waiter's attention. If you need to blow your nose or get something out of your teeth, excuse yourself from the table and take care of the matter in the restroom.

6 Be affectionate with your fiancée—but not too affectionate. Hold hands. Put your arm around her. Gaze adoringly at her. Give her a peck on the lips. You want your future in-laws to see how much you love her. You don't, however, want them to picture you in bed with her, so don't take this approach too far.

7. Write a note to your fiancée's parents after the get-together. If they took you out for a meal, thank them. If you took them out or you had them over for cocktails, tell them what a great time you had. Use real paper and pen, not e-mail.

GET THE PARTY STARTED

Once upon a time, the bride's family threw some sort of stuffy engagement soiree. They still might, but these days anyone can host such a party. Engaged couples themselves often throw their own laid-back bashes as a way to simultaneously announce their good news and get their respective friends to start interacting. Invitations can go out via e-mail, phone, or regular mail. And the party itself can run the gamut from an early evening wine-and-cheese affair at home to a dinner gathering at a fine restaurant. Just remember that everyone you invite will assume a wedding invitation is on the way, so choose carefully.

PARTY POINTERS

If you aren't used to parties that don't involve kegs, here are a few basic tips to help you sail smoothly through your engagement party.

* Look sharp. Consult with your fiancée—and with the host of the party—about what to wear. When in doubt, overdress.

* Don't gorge yourself silly. You may be nervous, in which case the temptation to hide by the food table is understandable. But if you spend the whole time shoveling cheese and crackers in your mouth, you'll look like a pig and leave guests wondering why you didn't speak to them.

* Mingle, mingle, mingle. Sure, you want to catch up with your college buddies, but an engagement party is your opportunity to win over your bride's friends and family. Ignoring them won't get you anywhere.

* Divide and conquer. Don't be afraid to leave your bride's side. While you're schmoozing with her friends and family, she can do the same with yours. That way all of the guests will leave the party impressed.

* Act as if you're running for office. When you meet people, give them a firm handshake, maintain eye contact, and smile. And don't forget their names—when you're introduced, repeat the name out loud to help you remember.

* Keep one hand free. If you've got a drink in one hand and a plate of food in the other, you've got a problem. Your right hand should always be available for shaking.

* Hydrate yourself—not with liquor. Make sure you drink plenty of water. Alcohol is not taboo, but don't overdo it.

* Keep the conversation light. Don't bring up politics or religion. Getting into a brawl is not the best way for you to make a good impression.

* Be unfailingly polite. If there are bartenders or servers, say please and thank you. Thank guests for coming, thank guests for offering congratulations, and thank the host or hostess for throwing the shindig.

Chapter Two

First Steps

You're ready to get started on the actual planning. Great. But hold on. Before you begin checking out wedding singers and picking out a tux, there are a few basic steps to get out of the way. Some are exciting—like picking a time and place to tie the knot. Others—such as figuring out your finances—can be excruciating. Just keep reminding yourself that somewhere down the line there's a honeymoon waiting for you. These planning preliminaries are like the broccoli you have to force down before you get to indulge in dessert.

TALK THE TALK

You may think you've been through a lot with your new fiancée, but the months leading up to a wedding can be a tense time. Before you even begin to plan, sit down with your bride and talk—about talking.

* Agree to keep communicating in the months (not to mention years and decades) ahead, even when you're feeling stressed, angry, and resentful.

* Note that communicating means not only talking, but listening—and hearing what the other person has to say.

* Acknowledge that you're going to fight and disagree and want to throttle each other—and that that's completely healthy. (Note: To *actually* throttle each other is not healthy.)

* Accept and understand that compromise is key to wedding planning and marriage. Some couples choose to see a marriage counselor at this early stage—not because their relationship is in trouble, but because counseling can help them learn to open up and listen to each other.

MONEY MATTERS

Unfortunately, before you can dive into the details of planning your wedding, you've got to deal with that most unpleasant of questions: How much money are you going to spend?

If you're like most couples, no one is going to be happy to spend the gross domestic product of a small country on your wedding festivities. In fact, the first thing you'll need to figure out is who will actually be paying for the event. Determining how the costs will be shared, and by whom, is a tricky business. The bride's parents traditionally pay for the bulk of the wedding, but expecting them to do so is simply unacceptable in this day and age. Note, too, that if your parents want to pay for the wedding, such an offer could be insulting to the bride's family. If you and your bride want to shoulder the costs yourselves, you may cause your parents or hers to feel left out. On the other hand, the folks may expect you two to pay for your own wedding—after all, you're mature enough to get married, so you're hardly little kids anymore.

In other words, this issue is something you need to talk about openly and honestly. You and your bride should have a heart-to-heart first—discussing both families' financial situations and your own expectations about dividing the costs—and then get both sets of parents involved in the conversation. Deciding to share costs (in some proportion) among your parents, her parents, and yourselves may be the best bet. Once you've figured out who's going to write which checks, you'll be better able to decide how large those checks can be.

WHO PAYS FOR WHAT?

If you want to do things by the book—the old, outdated book—the bride and her parents pay for most of the wedding, while you and your parents cover a few of the extras, as the list on the following pages shows. Under no circumstances should you shove this list in front of your fiancée's family and announce, "Look what you have to pay for." It merely represents the traditional breakdown of costs, one that you may choose to use as a general guideline—or completely ignore.

The groom and his family:

* Engagement ring

* Bride's wedding ring

* Rehearsal dinner

* Groom's wedding attire

* Marriage license

* Officiant's fee

* Bride's bouquet

* Corsages for mothers and grandmothers (yours and hers)

* Boutonnieres for the groom, groomsmen, and all fathers and grandfathers

* Gifts for the groomsmen

* Wedding present for the bride (if you're exchanging gifts)

* Honeymoon

The bride and her family:

* Groom's wedding ring

* Bride's wedding attire

* Stationery (wedding invitations, thank-you notes, ceremony programs, place cards for reception, etc.)

* Bouquets for the bridesmaids and flower girls

* Fee for the ceremony site

* Reception site, food, and drink

* Flowers and decorations for the ceremony and reception

* Rental items for the ceremony and reception

* Music for the ceremony and reception

* Photography and videography

* Transportation for the bridal party

* Gifts for the bridesmaids

* Wedding favors for guests

* Wedding gift for the groom

As you can see, in this traditional division, the costs are heavily weighted on the bride's side. In recent years, it's become more common for both families to share the costs evenly—or for the bride and groom to pay for everything themselves. If you and your bride are paying, you may want to chat with a financial planner who can help you set some realistic expectations about what you can afford. You don't want to throw the most luxurious wedding the world has ever seen—and then end up eating ramen noodles for the next decade to make up for it.

MONEY-SAVING TIPS: OVERALL WEDDING PLANNING

You might want to sit down for this: The average cost of a wedding in the United States is more than $22,000. As you begin to figure out what *your* budget is, here are some ways to keep costs down.

* Get married off-season. The most popular—and most expensive—part of the year to tie the knot is May through October. Consider having your wedding during a month that doesn't fall in this peak season.

* Have a cocktail reception with drinks, hors d'oeuvres, and a cake. There's no rule that you must have a full sit-down meal for a wedding. (If you opt for this approach, be sure to make it clear on the invitation, so guests aren't expecting to be fed dinner.)

* Hold a daytime reception. Because most people opt for Saturday night, many venues charge less for a daytime event, such as brunch or lunch.

* Look into having a buffet for the reception meal instead of a served repast, as the former approach is often less expensive.

* Get married during the week instead of on the weekend. Be aware, though, that some guests may not be able to attend if you take this approach.

* Stay away from such holidays as Valentine's Day and Mother's Day, when flowers are more expensive.

* Keep the guest list small. The amount that you spend on food and drink will be greatly affected by the number of people eating and imbibing. Also, the greater the head count, the more invitations and centerpieces you'll need to order.

Wedding Budget Planner

Once you've figured out a total budget for the wedding, you can decide how much money you've got available for specific areas. Your wedding is a highly personal affair, but generally speaking, you should plan to spend about 50 percent of the overall budget on the reception, 10 percent on flowers and other decorations, 10 percent on music, 10 percent on photography and videography,

10 percent on attire for you and the bride (plus your bride's hair and makeup appointments), and 10 percent on other elements, such as the stationery, ceremony, transportation, favors, and additional gifts. As you estimate costs, be sure to account for gratuities and taxes, which often are not included in fees quoted to you. The following worksheet can help you establish—and, hopefully, stick to—a wedding budget. (Don't forget to save money for the honeymoon, which is a separate cost not included in this wedding budget planner.)

Element	Estimate	Actual	Deposit	Balance
RECEPTION (50%)				
Venue fee				
Food/caterer				
Bar/corkage fee				
Champagne/wine				
Cake/cake-cutting fee				
Rental items/equipment				
Parking				
Coat check				
Tips				
Wedding consultant				
Other				
Subtotal				
MUSIC (10%)				
Musicians for ceremony				
DJ/Band				
Subtotal				

(continued on next page)

Element	Estimate	Actual	Deposit	Balance
FLOWERS/DECORATIONS (10%)				
Flowers/decorations for ceremony site				
Bouquet for bride				
Maid of honor's bouquet				
Attendants' bouquets				
Toss bouquet				
Corsages				
Boutonnieres				
Flower girls' baskets				
Reception centerpieces				
Other reception flowers/ decorations				
Subtotal				
PHOTOGRAPHY/VIDEOGRAPHY (10%)				
Photography package/fee				
Wedding album (if not part of package)				
Additional albums				
Additional prints				
Negatives				
Videography package/fee				
Additional videos				

Element	Estimate	Actual	Deposit	Balance
Disposable cameras and corresponding costs for developing film				
Subtotal				
ATTIRE/GROOMING (10%)				
Bride's gown				
Alterations to gown				
Bride's veil/headpiece				
Bride's shoes				
Jewelry and other bridal accessories				
Rehearsal dinner attire for bride				
Bride's going-away outfit				
Bride's hair/makeup/nails				
Groom's wedding attire				
Groom's shoes				
Groom's accessories (tie, vest or cummerbund, cuff links and studs, etc.)				
Groom's rehearsal dinner attire				
Groom's going-away attire				
Subtotal				

(continued on next page)

Element	Estimate	Actual	Deposit	Balance
ADDITIONAL EXPENSES (10%)				
STATIONERY				
Wedding invitations				
Wedding announcements				
Save-the-date cards				
Thank-you notes				
Ceremony programs				
Seating cards				
Fee for calligrapher				
Postage for invitations, response cards, thank-you notes, etc.				
Other items				
Subtotal				
CEREMONY				
Site fee				
Fee/donation for officiant				
Ceremonial objects (goblet, unity candle, etc.)				
Marriage license				
Wedding rings				
Other				
Subtotal				

Element	Estimate	Actual	Deposit	Balance
TRANSPORTATION				
Rented vehicles for the bride, groom, immediate family, and wedding party				
Tips for drivers				
Guest shuttle				
Subtotal				
GIFTS				
Favors for guests				
Welcome baskets for out-of-towners				
Gifts for attendants				
Thank-you gifts for parents				
Bride's and groom's presents to each other				
Subtotal				
OTHER EVENTS				
Bridesmaids' luncheon				
Rehearsal dinner (site, food, drinks, invitations, etc.)				
Subtotal				
MISCELLANEOUS				
TOTAL				

COVER YOUR BASES: WEDDING INSURANCE

It isn't something anyone wants to think about at a joyous time, but weddings sometimes need to be postponed. If a major storm strikes, for example, flights might be canceled, preventing the majority of guests from being able to get to the event. Or the bride or groom may be forced, at the last minute, to relocate to another state for professional reasons.

To prepare for the worst-case scenarios, the host of the wedding may want to consider purchasing wedding insurance. Policies differ, but they can cover the loss of nonrefundable deposits for sites and service providers should the planned wedding have to be called off for certain reasons (if you or the bride gets cold feet, however, you're out of luck).

Some wedding insurance policies provide liability coverage in case someone is injured during the wedding or afterward as a result of it. If a wedding guest drives under the influence and tragedy ensues, the host of the event could be held legally responsible. (In an ideal world, your friends and relatives would conduct themselves like the intelligent, sophisticated adults they are, but unless you're not serving alcohol, you can't count on this.) Some policies also cover property damage caused by guests or vendors. If you've got an uncle who was famous for trashing hotel rooms during his days as a drummer in a heavy metal band, this is for you. Again, all policies are different, so it is important to shop around and understand exactly what is covered and what is not.

SETTING THE DATE AND TIME

Wedding venues book up far in advance, so you and your bride should figure out the when and where of the wedding as early as possible. Here are some questions to ask yourselves when deciding upon a time and date.

How much time do we want to give ourselves to plan the wedding? The less amount of time you give yourselves for the planning process, the more stress and pressure you're likely to feel as you attempt to get everything done. If you or your bride is dreaming of a formal wedding in which every detail must be perfect, it's a good idea to give yourself at least nine months, if not longer. Again, sites—and vendors, for that matter— book up far in advance (so if your bride is determined to get married at that French chateau she saw on her favorite reality dating show, you may be stuck waiting a lot longer).

What season strikes our fancy? If you and your fiancée have a favorite time of year, getting married then might make your wedding even more special. Bear in mind that if winter is your preferred season and many of your guests will be coming from far away, snowstorms could pose a problem. Consider, too, whether you want all or part of the event to be outdoors, and plan accordingly. And don't forget that if there are financial concerns, certain times of the year are pricier than others.

Is cost a consideration? Again, Saturday evening is the most expensive time to have a reception; mornings and afternoons are cheaper. Late spring, summer, and early fall are the most popular—and most costly—times of year to get married. (For more details about this issue, refer back to page 35.)

Do we want to have our wedding over a holiday weekend? There are pros and cons to scheduling a wedding over a holiday, such as Thanksgiving, Christmas, or New Year's. On the pro side, many people have time off and won't need to take a vacation day to attend; that said, they may already have other plans. Plus, airfares tend to be higher at these peak travel times, so getting to the wedding could be more expensive for traveling guests. Note also that the cost of throwing the wedding will most likely be higher during such times, as holidays are popular wedding dates. Valentine's Day is another pricey time to get married.

Are there any religious or family conflicts? Make sure you consider religious holidays that might keep guests of various faiths from attending. Beware of other family obligations, even if there's no direct conflict on the date itself. For instance, if your sibling is getting married a month before you, some relatives may pick just one wedding to attend. And don't forget that classic American holiday: Super Bowl Sunday. If you hold your wedding that afternoon or evening, your male friends will never forgive you. And if they do show up, don't be surprised to find a lot of tiny TVs drowning out your vows.

Where do we want to go on our honeymoon? If you have your heart set on a certain destination and you wish to go on your honeymoon right after the wedding, you may want to investigate the optimal times of year for visiting the location and then weigh this factor into your decision. Certain months will obviously have better weather, while others may be less expensive times to travel.

PICKING THE PERFECT PLACE

When considering where to have your wedding (both the ceremony and the reception), ask yourselves the following basic questions.

Are we indoor or outdoor people? This is tougher than it sounds. Maybe your ideal setting for a wedding is a botanical garden on a sunny summer day, with a cool breeze blowing through the air. You're an outdoor person, right? Not so fast. Close your eyes and picture that same wedding—with a sudden rainstorm drenching everyone there. If you're starting to hyperventilate at the thought, you may be better suited to an indoor wedding after all.

Will everyone be able to make it? Getting married on the beach in Maui—or by an Elvis impersonator in Vegas—sounds swell, but will your friends and relatives be able to afford the trip, not to mention the time? You shouldn't sacrifice a dream wedding, but getting married near where you or your relatives live means more of your guests will be there.

How many people will we have? Before you look at specific sites, you need a rough idea of how many guests—relatives, friends, coworkers—you plan to invite. (For details on how to put together a guest list, see page 48.)

How formal do we want the reception to be? Are you thinking formal, black-tie affair or casual, laid-back bash? Deciding upon the tone of the event will allow you to narrow down the list of sites to visit.

Will our ideal officiant go for it? If you already know who you want to have perform the ceremony, be sure to check out the logistics with him/her. The officiant may not be able to travel far—or may have strict rules about where ceremonies can take place.

A Step-by-Step Guide to Choosing a Site

1. Call ahead. Ask what dates are available and how many people the place can hold before actually going to visit a place. This can save you loads of aggravation (and gas money).

2. Hit the pavement. Once you've determined that a site's availability and capacity meet your needs, make an appointment with the coordinator/manager to visit the place in person. Note the overall style, check out the views, and take a look at how much parking is available.

3. Find out what's included. Some sites have in-house catering and wait staff and a standard set of tables, chairs, linens, etc. In other cases—parks, some halls and clubs, and presumably your families' homes, for instance—you'll need to rent such items as seating and china, as well as hire outside caterers and servers.

4. Ask if you can see a reception site when it's actually set up for a wedding or similar occasion. If this request is granted, dress appropriately, be unobtrusive, and take a quick peek— no lingering.

5. If you're thinking about having any part of your wedding outdoors, make sure there's a clear backup plan that's easy to put into place in case of rain, freak hailstorms, and the like.

6. If you plan to marry in a public place (a beach or park, for example), ask about any permit requirements.

7. If other weddings are happening on the same day or night, be certain they won't interfere with yours; find out how this type of situation is handled, and make sure you're comfortable with the answer.

8. If there's a site coordinator, be sure you're comfortable working with him or her and that this person is responsive to your needs and wishes. You may be spending a lot of time together in the months ahead.

Chapter Three

Picking the Players

Deciding who exactly will share the day with you is one of the most challenging parts of planning the event. This is the stage during which couples often begin to argue, cry, and wonder if it's too late to elope. While it may not be too late, consider this: The two of you will have plenty of time alone together in the years to come. Your wedding day gives friends and family the chance to come together, gaze adoringly at you, and pay up on all those bets they made that you'd never commit.

GUEST LIST GROUND RULES

Unless you're loaded, you probably aren't going to be able to include every single person you've ever met. Start by figuring out how many people you can invite—based on your budget and, if you already have your hearts set on a venue, the number of people that the site can hold. Once the magic number has been determined, there are a few different approaches for establishing how many guests each "party" gets to invite.

1. All lists are created equal. In this scenario, the total number of guests is divided by three. You and your fiancée together get a third, and the parents on each side get a third. Family members and relatives belong on your parents' lists (regardless of which approach you take). And if your parents invite their hideous friend Bertha, suck it up. It's their third to do with as they wish. Like it or not, you don't get veto power.

2. Money talks. In this approach, whoever is paying for the bulk of the wedding gets to invite the bulk of the guests. So, if you and your bride are emptying your bank accounts to throw the wedding to end all weddings, you can invite more of your own friends and limit your parents' guest lists. Similarly, if the bride's family is footing the bill, be prepared for them to get a bigger portion of the head count.

3. Size matters. This approach involves dividing up the guest list according to family size. For instance, if your family is triple the size of your bride's, you get three times as many guests on your list. Of course, if the people paying have a small family, they're not likely to jump at this option. You might start by dividing the list evenly and then giving a few extra spots to the larger family.

MAKING THE CUT

Once you and your bride have your allotted number of guests, jot down everyone you might want to include on your list. Consider friends, coworkers, drinking buddies, you name it. After you've completed this wish list, you'll probably need to whittle it down to hit the target number; inevitably, you'll need to nix some people you really wanted to invite. Here are some tried-and-true methods for getting through this process while offending as few people as possible.

* Once you start inviting a few coworkers, you open the floodgates. Consider not including the people you work with. Or invite only those in your immediate department (be sure to include your boss). Whatever you decide, do it across the board. A sure way to find yourself in hot water is to invite some people from a group but not others (and you don't want that one person you left out to become your boss a month later).

* Know that just because you were invited to someone's wedding doesn't mean you have to reciprocate. If a couple of years have passed and you've drifted apart, you're off the hook.

* Unless your guests are in serious, long-term relationships, don't invite them to bring dates. If anyone asks, just explain that you have to limit the guest list, so you're asking single people to come alone. Besides, weddings are the perfect singles events.

* Draw a line in the family tree. Your immediate family makes the cut. So do first cousins, aunts and uncles, and grandparents.

Unless they're virtual strangers, include stepsiblings and step-grandparents as well. But if you want to invite second cousins, you should be prepared to invite *all* of your second cousins—unless you want to create a permanent family rift.

* X the exes. Unless your fiancée has become buddies with your ex-girlfriends, leave them off the list. Anything that makes your bride uncomfortable at her own wedding should be avoided.

* Get rid of the kids. It's perfectly acceptable to have an adults-only event or to limit the kiddie list to nieces and nephews and, perhaps, children of the wedding party members. But here, too, it's got to be an across-the-board policy. You can't invite one friend's cherubs and tell another that her hellions aren't welcome.

* Make an A-list and a B-list. If people from the A-list can't attend, you can start sending invitations to the B-listers—as long as you do so at least four weeks in advance of the wedding (otherwise these invitees will know they were second-tier and be insulted anyway).

THE BEST MAN

Being the maid of honor at a wedding is a gigantic responsibility. Being the best man is, by comparison, a piece of cake. There are only a few basic tasks that best men typically do across the board:

1. Plan the bachelor party
2. Attend the rehearsal and rehearsal dinner
3. Participate in a photo session for formal wedding portraits

4. Hold on to the bride's ring until the appropriate point in the ceremony

5. Stand next to the groom and look awkward throughout the ceremony

6. Make the first toast during the reception

That's the bare minimum. If you've picked someone highly organized and responsible, you may want to assign him additional tasks, such as:

7. Help get you dressed and to the wedding site on time

8. Bring the marriage license to the wedding

9. Sign the marriage license as an official witness

10. Make sure any last-minute payments are made on the wedding day (not with his own money, however)

11. Make sure that all groomsmen make the proper arrangements for renting formalwear

12. Ensure that any rented attire is returned on time

MAKING THE RIGHT CHOICE

The best man can be a friend, sibling, cousin—even your father. If you're lucky, this is a no-brainer. If you've got just one brother whom you trust and love like, oh, a brother, stop thinking. He's your best man. If you've got a longtime best buddy and confidante, he's your best man. But what if you've got one of each? Or twelve brothers? Here are some pointers to picking the best man—without offending your other friends and family.

Divide and conquer. Got two brothers? Two best friends? Make them *both* best men, and divvy up their duties. If taking this approach salvages your relationships, it's worth a few stares from the traditionalists in the audience.

Guru Grooms on...

The Best Man

"Our wedding ceremony was somewhat nontraditional, so we didn't have a best man or maid of honor or any of that stuff. In the end I think that worked out well; we avoided the stress of having to choose a wedding party and organize special events and all that, and the people who would have otherwise been in the wedding party were free to just enjoy the party."

—*Steve, 30, Los Angeles*

Avoid the reflex choice. If your brother gets panic attacks and collapses in a heap whenever he has to speak in front of a crowd, he'll most likely understand—and be eternally grateful—if you give the job of best man to someone else (though you should probably run the idea by him first). And if your best friend used to date your fiancée and never really got over her, you may want to give him a low-profile role in the wedding. Above all, pick someone responsible. Your best man is supposed to worry about you during your wedding—not the other way around.

Blood is thicker than water. When in doubt, choose family over friends. Honestly, any pal will understand if you ask your brother to be your best man. But your sibling might not be so supportive if you pick that guy you met three years ago while getting drunk and watching *Simpsons* reruns.

Go for the best speechwriter. If you're deciding between brothers or between close friends, consider this criterion. Hopefully, all of your potential candidates can be trusted to hold a wedding ring and make it to the ceremony on time. So the most important remaining responsibility is giving that toast. Choose someone who you think can strike the right balance of wit and poignancy, not someone who will bring out the offensive jokes.

Steer clear of danger. Avoid the drunkard, the perennial latecomer, the stoner, the flake, and any other disasters-in-waiting—even if that description fits your best friend.

THE GROOMSMEN

What, exactly, does a groomsman do? Not much. Most intelligent chimpanzees could fill the role. Traditional groomsmen duties include:

1. Attend the rehearsal and rehearsal dinner

2. Serve as ushers during the ceremony, which involves offering an arm to the women, showing all guests to their seats, and handing out programs

3. Roll out the runner for the bride to walk on, if necessary

4. Stand up front during the ceremony

5. Escort the bridesmaids during the recessional

6. Participate in a photo session for formal wedding portraits

The classic rule is that there be one usher per every fifty guests (to make the seating process go smoothly). If you're trying to keep the number of bridesmaids and groomsmen equal or relatively close and that leaves you short on people to usher, your groomsmen will be mowed down by the eager-to-be-seated masses. There is a solution to this problem: Designate other close friends or relatives to serve as extra ushers (as opposed to being full-fledged stand-at-the-altar groomsmen). This tactic also presents you with the opportunity to give others a part in your wedding. (Incidentally, you should note that you're not required to have an equal number of groomsmen and bridesmaids.)

DIPLOMATIC DECISIONS

The selection of groomsmen affords yet another opportunity to offend friends and family. Once again, here are a few ways to minimize the damage.

Brothers belong. Unless you're bitter enemies who aren't on speaking terms, your male siblings are automatic groomsmen. And if you *are* bitter enemies, now's the time to get over it.

Family trumps friends. This rule can actually be a lifesaver. You've likely got far more male friends than male relatives, so if you don't want to hurt your friends' feelings by leaving them out, you can always limit your groomsmen to brothers and cousins. Or fill the ranks with *her* brothers.

Speaking of her brothers — it's *your* call. You are not, under any circumstances, obligated to include your bride's family members in the wedding party. If you've come to like them, it's a nice gesture, but your own friends and family can—and should—come first.

Get the excluded involved. Friends and family who didn't fit as groomsmen can still take part in the ceremony in other ways—by giving a reading, for example, or escorting your grandmother down the aisle.

Chapter Four

Getting Busy
Planning Ahead for Your Wedding Day

Many of the finer details of wedding planning can wait until the last couple of months (not minutes, months). But some tasks need to be tackled far ahead of time to avert any last-minute disasters.

THE CEREMONY

Religion can be a touchy subject, to say the least. So it's a good idea to deal with the question of whether to have a civil or religious ceremony as early as possible. If everyone's in agreement, count your blessings and move on. If your parents or your future in-laws are pulling you in different directions, you and your fiancée need to come to an agreement and present a united front. Remember: You want to make your families happy, but in the end, it's your wedding.

THE RELIGIOUS ROUTE: CHOOSING AN OFFICIANT

Once you've established what type of ceremony you'll be having, you can start looking for an officiant. If you're having a religious wedding, here are some guidelines for this process.

* First, consider the obvious. If you and your bride belong to the same church, temple, or mosque—and you're not getting married on the other side of the country—simply set up a meeting with the appropriate person and ask him/her to do the honors. You've got it easy. Go ahead—feel smug.

* Check for family ties. Much of the time, parents already have someone in mind to perform their children's weddings—often a relative or family friend, if not their longtime local clergyperson. Your bride may have forgotten the name of the rabbi who performed her bat mitzvah, but her parents are sure to remember—and might still play bridge with him every week.

* Remember: location, location, location. If you're thinking of getting married in a house of worship that you're not familiar with, ask to meet with the minister or rabbi there. He or she may be a stranger, but you've got some time to get to know each other. Note that some houses of worship will not let you bring in an outside officiant, so before you commit to a ceremony site, find out what the rules are. You should also inquire as to whether

there are any requirements that you need to fulfill in order to marry there.

* Let your fingers do the walking. So, you're getting married in a hotel in the city you moved to a couple of years ago—and you haven't gone to a religious service since grade school. This is why you're starting early. Pick up a phone book, and attend a slew of services. When you hear a sermon that you like, set up a meeting with the person who delivered it. Continue this process until you and your soon-to-be-spouse hit it off with someone. There's an added benefit to starting from scratch: It can be pretty awkward at a wedding when the officiant goes on for half an hour about watching the bride grow up—and then has nothing to say about the groom. This way, you get to know the officiant together, as a couple.

* When speaking with an officiant, politely ask some tough questions. If you intend to personalize your ceremony—by adding readings or cultural/ethnic elements or writing your own vows—find out if this person is on board. He or she may not allow modifications to the service, in which case you may need to keep looking for the right person to perform the ceremony.

CHOOSING A CIVIL OFFICIANT

* If you're going with a civil ceremony, you've got a few options when it comes to selecting an officiant. A judge or justice of the peace are the most common choices, but mayors and other elected officials can often preside over weddings; in some areas, a notary public will suffice. Best of all, there are some towns in which anyone can get a temporary license to perform a wedding ceremony, which means you could have a mutual friend do the job. Check with the local town clerk's office where you're getting married to find out the specific rules.

* Just as you would with a minister or rabbi, you need to have a frank discussion with any officiant you're considering for a civil ceremony. Key points to cover include:

  * Is this person legally able and willing to perform the marriage ceremony in the place you want to hold it?

  * Does he/she have a problem with any elements you want to include in the ceremony, including readings and personalized vows?

  * Will he/she give some kind of introductory speech?

* Make sure that you and your bride feel comfortable with the officiant before deciding to have this person perform your ceremony.

MIXED BLESSINGS

If you and your soul mate are of different faiths, you've got a lot to figure out down the road: how to deal with holidays, how to raise children, and how to keep both sets of parents from bursting into tears anytime the subject of religion comes up. Good luck. But when it comes to your wedding ceremony, you've got a few ways to deal with your differences.

* Hold an interfaith ceremony. In this case, an officiant from each faith performs a part of the ceremony. This is often the easiest way to deal with interfaith issues without upsetting anyone. But don't assume that the officiants you're considering will automatically participate in such a service. Some won't, so be prepared to keep looking or come up with an alternate solution.

* Hold two separate ceremonies. Obviously, you can't have two full-fledged weddings without losing your sanity—and your life savings. But a small, family-only ceremony the day before the one with the big audience and reception may reassure your family (or hers) that you're not abandoning their religion.

* Choose one religion for the ceremony. When it comes to your wedding, a religious ceremony may be vital to one of you and not the other. Just make sure to be completely up front with the officiant. Explain that you're of two different faiths and that no one is converting. If you're Protestant, you don't want a priest at your wedding telling everyone how wonderful it is that you've decided to raise your kids in a Catholic household when you have yet to make that decision. You should also be aware that some officiants may not be willing to marry two people of different faiths—even if you're not incorporating elements of the other faith into the ceremony; if you're considering this type of scenario, be sure to discuss it in your first conversation with any prospective officiant.

* Settle on a civil service. If all else fails, you might want to avoid a religious ceremony. That said, just because you choose the civil route does not mean you need to remove all spirituality from your ceremony. You could have a close friend or family member read a passage from the Bible; you might also be able to incorporate certain rituals, such as the Jewish breaking of the glass. Here, too, you'll need to make sure the officiant you're considering is open to the elements you want.

CULTURE CLASH

In all likelihood, your rabbi, priest, imam, or judge has a set blueprint for the wedding ceremony. But hopefully that blueprint leaves room for modifications; as previously mentioned, it's important to clarify this matter with any officiant you're considering. Early in the planning process, sit down with your bride—and consult both of your families—to decide if there are any ethnic or cultural traditions you want to weave into your wedding. You or your bride may wish to wear traditional clothing that reflects your heritage. You may want to include readings from books important to her culture or yours. You may want to have decorations that celebrate your ethnicity.

In any case, once you get to the reception, it's your show. Nearly every culture has traditional ethnic wedding dances—the Jewish hora, the Italian tarantella, or the Greek Kalamatianos, for example—which all guests can enjoy, even if they have absolutely no idea what they're doing. Serving ethnic food is another way to work your backgrounds into the day. Some traditions seem to transcend culture. Lifting the bride and groom in chairs used to be a strictly Jewish tradition; these days it's incorporated into plenty of secular and Christian weddings.

Writing Your Own Vows

If you've been to a few weddings, you've probably seen it. The bride gives a richly detailed history of the couple's relationship, reflects on how her guy was there for her in tough times, and recounts how he makes her laugh. She talks about growing old together, about being best friends and soul mates, about destiny and fate and true love. It's pure poetry—by the time she finishes, even the most macho guests are weeping.

Then it's the groom's turn. "Um," he begins, "you're the best. I never dreamed I'd find a woman who likes football. Uh, I love you. Like, *a lot.*"

This is the reason to think carefully about whether you want to write your own vows. Even if the differences between the bride's and groom's words aren't so pronounced, they're rarely balanced; one person's vows are always longer, or more emotional, or simply better written than the other's, which leaves the bride and groom embarrassed and guests squirming in their seats.

Still, plenty of couples are determined to personalize their vows. If you're one of them, here are a few ground rules to help the process go as smoothly as possible.

* As mentioned earlier, consult your officiant first. The officiant may have guidelines about what areas your vows can cover. Or there may be words you *must* include in order for your vows to be legally binding.

* Mutually agree on a time limit—and stick to it. Short and sweet is always the best bet. You and your bride have a lifetime to whisper gushy endearments to each other.

* Decide on the tone—together. Just as awkward as vows that are of vastly different lengths are ones that are vastly different in mood (one person's words are moving and eloquent, while the other's vows consist of jokes). Before you begin writing, agree on how mushy you're going to get. And if you're a comedian—or you like to think you are—this is one of those moments to keep your comic instincts in check. Bawdy stories and dirty jokes are always a bad idea at a wedding.

* Be specific. "I love you" is nice to hear; ditto "You make me happy." But you're marrying this person, so those sentiments are pretty much a given. What is it that sets your bride apart from every other woman you've ever known? If everything you're writing sounds like a cliché, try telling the story of your first date or the moment you first realized you were in love, or just relating an anecdote that illustrates who she is.

* Remember: They're called vows for a reason. Don't forget to include a promise to love and cherish and care for your bride for the rest of your life.

* Rehearse. If you've written the most beautiful vows ever uttered and then can't remember a word, it's not going to do you much

good. Looking down at your feet and mumbling incoherently won't go over well either. Practice speaking slowly and clearly while gazing adoringly at a photo of your bride. And just in case you get stage fright, write your vows on a few note cards and shove them in your tux pocket. Yes, it looks lame to read your vows, but it looks worse to stand there stammering and red-faced when your mind goes blank. Besides, just knowing that they're in your pocket can help boost your confidence.

* Find an impartial judge and practice in front of him/her. If you and your bride each read your vows to a mutual friend, he/she can alert you to any potential problems—differences in tone or length—well before the wedding day.

RECEPTION MUSIC: A NOTE-WORTHY SUBJECT

Of all the planning areas traditionally under the bride's control, the one you might want to get involved with most is the reception music. After all, if you're not in love with your bride's choice of floral arrangements, you'll probably be able to forge ahead. But if the band sounds like an *American Idol* reject or your DJ tells X-rated jokes, your guests might decide to crash someone else's wedding.

WHO TO HIRE?
Your first task: Decide between a DJ and a band. Disc jockeys typically cost less than bands. And with a DJ, you pretty much know what you're getting: Songs will sound the way you've always known and loved them. A bad band, however, can butcher the classics; plus, if the band has only a male singer, certain songs may not be an option or could sound pretty strange. On the other hand, a band brings a higher energy level to the party. And, right or wrong, a band is seen as a classier choice. Whichever way you go, here are some tips to make sure you hit the right notes.

The Reception: The Big Picture

How much you participate in planning the details of the wedding reception will be a matter for you and your bride to decide. However, there are certain larger elements that the two of you should work out together, such as picking the place and style of the event—both of which were discussed in chapter two. Remember that the type of reception you have (brunch vs. dinner; buffet vs. served food; cocktails, hors d'oeuvres, and cake vs. full meal) will have a big effect on costs. You might also want to weigh in on the menu, types of beverages to be served, and cake flavor if you have any preferences.

* Ask around. Friends and relatives are happy to go on about the amazing band or DJ that played at cousin so-and-so's shindig. And for once, don't ignore your parents' advice—after all, the music has to appeal to your generation *and* theirs.

* See them do their thing. Ask bands and DJs you're considering if you can take in a live performance to get a better idea of how they really operate. Ideally, you should observe them at an actual wedding reception so you can get a feel for their rapport with the guests in that type of setting. (If you're granted this request, dress appropriately and be inconspicuous.)

* A band or DJ may not feel comfortable letting you crash a wedding performance. In such a situation, ask for a video of the candidates in question performing at a wedding so you can still get some kind of feel for not only ability, but style and demeanor. If this request is denied, go elsewhere. Don't trust a CD: Not only is the sound quality unreliable, but you won't know if the members are performing with scowls on their faces or wearing torn

jeans and T-shirts. If you're going through an agency and you're basing your decision on a videotape, make sure that the band you saw is the one you're actually getting before signing anything.

* Remember: It's a *wedding.* Don't hire a band or DJ you saw at that amazing club minutes before you passed out. You want people who have done many, many weddings and know the routine.

* Get a sample playlist. This gives you an idea of the sort of music the band or DJ specializes in. If the list is filled with swing while you want disco, consider it a warning sign.

* If you're interviewing a band, make sure the group knows any songs you consider vital—the Chicken Dance, Hava Nagilah, or the ballad that you've decided on for your first spin on the dance floor. If the band members don't know something you consider critical, will they learn it? If you're dealing with a DJ, find out if the desired songs are in his/her collection; if not, will the DJ obtain them or play them if you provide the CDs? If anyone balks, consider moving on to someone else.

* Don't concentrate solely on the dance music. Will the band/DJ play during the cocktail hour, and if so, what kind of tunes? What will the band/DJ play during dinner?

* Find out how many breaks the band/DJ takes and how this absence is filled. Silence may be golden—but not during a reception. A disc jockey should be able to keep some tunes going while he/she takes a breather. And the band should have enough members so that someone's always there to play while the others are hitting the restrooms—or, as a backup, have some recorded music to switch on instead.

* Find out if the bandleader/DJ is willing to act as emcee, introducing you as you make your grand entrance as husband and wife and announcing such highlights as the cake-cutting and

Tuning Up

After you've decided who to go with, give your music provider a list of songs you'd like played during the reception. You should also hand over a list of songs you don't want to hear. And if the bandleader/DJ will be introducing you and your bride and the wedding party, make sure he/she knows how to pronounce each person's name.

bouquet toss. If not, is there a wedding coordinator at the reception site or someone else who can take on this responsibility?

* Don't be afraid to be strict. If your nightmare is a DJ who decides to test out his stand-up comedy act during your reception, be clear: No banter.

* Even if the band/DJ was recommended to you, get three references before hiring. If a music provider won't give you these, move on to the next candidate.

THE WRITTEN WORD

Once you've decided on a band/DJ, get a written contract. It is advisable that contracts include, but not necessarily be limited to, the following:

* Date and times the band/DJ will perform, including the exact arrival time for setting up and the number of hours the band/DJ will perform

* Exact location of the event where the band/DJ will perform (include address)

* Total number of people who will perform at your event

* All musical instruments to be played (if you're hiring a band)

* Names of each and every music provider being hired—and alternates in case of emergency

* Mention of any equipment needed, as well as who must supply it

* Notation that the bandleader/DJ will perform emcee duties, if this is part of the deal

* Any specific songs that the band/DJ has agreed to play at the event

* Agreement that the band/DJ will do its best to fulfill other requests for specific songs if you haven't selected all the music for reception highlights by the time of the contract signing

* Complete account of fees, including overtime charges and any other fees

* Number of breaks the band/DJ will take and whether recorded music will be played during those periods

* Description of the attire to be worn by the band members/DJ

* Complete payment schedule and amounts

* Policy for cancellation/refunds

SPECTATOR SPORTS

Sometimes there are reasons women are traditionally responsible for certain areas. When it comes to picking floral arrangements, for

example, most men have an attention span of approximately thirty-seven seconds. Listed here are areas that the bride may prefer to handle on her own. However, if she wants some help and input, don't leave her feeling like she's in this alone. Suck it up, tag along to meet with various vendors, and politely defer to her wise judgment. She'll appreciate you for it. And, of course, if you want to participate in the plans for any of these areas, go ahead—it's your wedding, too.

* Flowers

* Stationery (including wedding invitations, announcements, place cards, and thank-you notes)

* Ceremony music

* Photography and videography

* Menu/beverages/cake

* Rental items (table linens, china, tents, etc.)

* Favors

 Guru Grooms on...

Wedding Invitations

"We were planning a relatively formal reception, and my mother-in-law-to-be knew that invitations traditionally didn't include a response card to mail back. The idea is that the recipient is supposed to write back an original note accepting or declining the invitation. We got plenty of original notes from guests—not expressing joy at our pending union, but rather regret that they lost the response card. Other people didn't respond by the RSVP deadline because they kept looking in vain for the card. Other people called to tell us that whoever we hired to do the invitations had erred by omitting the response card. All in all, an invitation disaster."

—Len, 37, Philadelphia

Chapter Five

The Clothes Make the Man

While your high school prom may have been the last shindig at which you got gussied up, there are no similarities between that event and your wedding. Not only will renting a cheap tux at the local shop simply not cut it, but there are many more decisions to make when it comes to your wedding attire—as your bride will no doubt remind you.

Things to Do: Wedding Attire

☐ Figure out what basic style best suits your wedding (discuss the matter with your bride)

☐ Call formalwear shops to set up appointments (not all require an appointment, but it's best to call ahead)

☐ Try on an endless array of options

☐ Purchase your wedding-day outfit, or make the necessary arrangements to rent a tux

☐ Obtain all of the following in addition to your suit/tux:

    ☐ shoes

    ☐ shirt

    ☐ cummerbund or vest

    ☐ tie or ascot

    ☐ cuff links and studs

    ☐ socks

☐ Decide what the groomsmen should wear, and let them know what they need to do

☐ Make sure your groomsmen go for their fittings or send their measurements when they're supposed to, or hand this task off to your best man

☐ Go for your own fittings, and have the necessary alterations made

☐ Pick up your tux or suit

☐ Break in your shoes if they're new by wearing them around the house for short periods

☐ If the outfit is rented, ask your best man or another trusted friend or family member to return it after the wedding

☐ Pass out from exhaustion

DRESS TO IMPRESS: THE GROOM

There was a time when men were expected to know nothing about fashion and clothing. Back then, putting on a simple black tux was enough. Alas, thanks to metrosexuals, *Queer Eye for the Straight Guy,* and approximately 380 men's magazines, life is no longer so simple.

Your first step is to narrow down your options by figuring out what style best suits your wedding. If you're getting married outdoors, you should also consider the climate. It's important to remember that there are no absolutes. It's your wedding, so the most important factor is personal taste. If you feel completely ridiculous wearing an ascot, for example, don't do it. That said, here's a quick breakdown of the five most popular options.

The Basic Black Tux: This classic attire is still the safest bet for a formal evening wedding. It's also appropriate for a semiformal evening event.

The Suit: Guys often feel required to don a tux, but a suit is the modern man's top choice for an informal daytime or evening wedding. For winter and autumn events, dark colors are usually worn; lighter shades can be sported in spring or summer.

The Morning Suit: For a formal daytime event, a cutaway or morning coat (see page 73) is the classic favorite, worn with a waistcoat and an ascot or tie.

White Tie: For evening weddings, white tie or full dress—an ensemble of black tailcoat (see page 72), black trousers, white shirt, white vest, and obviously, a white tie—is the ultimate statement in ultraformality.

Jacket and Tie: For a truly casual spring or summer wedding, it's perfectly acceptable to wear a blue blazer and khakis.

STYLE POINTS

That was easy, right? Wrong. You've still got a slew of decisions to make. You'll need to go to a formalwear shop and try on a variety of styles. Ask for help from the resident experts, who can let you know if a certain style is ill suited to your body type. But before you head out, here's a little help making sense of all the options out there.

JACKET JARGON

Single-breasted: This style of jacket has one row of buttons running down the front. One- or two-button single-breasted jackets generally look fine on any body type, but three- and four-button versions should be reserved for tall, slim men.

Double-breasted: As you've probably gathered, this style has two rows of buttons down the front—one to close the jacket, the other just for show. The jacket's slightly boxier shape can help hide a gut.

Tailcoat: This type of jacket is short in front, with two long tails in the back (it's like you're wearing a mullet, but without the relentless mocking). This is a very formal look for an evening wedding. Note, however, that it does not flatter short, squat men.

Cutaway/morning coat: Sloping gently from the waist in front to one broad tail in the back, this style works with any body type. Typically gray in color, it's traditionally worn with a wing-collared shirt, an ascot, and striped trousers—though you can replace the ascot with a tie if you want to look less like a nineteenth-century dandy. It's a popular option for a formal daytime wedding.

Dinner jacket: Single- or double-breasted, this resembles a traditional tux jacket, but is usually white or ivory and worn with black satin-striped pants. It's a fine formal substitute for a tux, especially worn in summer or in a warm climate, in the afternoon or evening.

LAPEL LINGO

When it comes to formal jackets, you're looking at a choice of three different lapels.

Peaked: This lapel features a point that projects upward and outward just below the collar line.

Notched: This style features a V-shaped cut that points inward, right where the collar and lapel meet on the jacket.

Shawl: This smooth, rounded lapel tapers gradually as it curves downward.

SHIRT COLLARS

Laydown/turndown: This is the basic kind of collar you see on a dress shirt worn with a suit, but it can also be worn with a tuxedo jacket. It's the least formal, but most comfortable, option. Similar to this style is the spread collar, which is a bit less pointed, sits a little higher on the neck, and is considered more formal.

Winged: A dressier choice, this type of collar stands up with pointed tips that fold downward. It goes best with an ascot or a bow tie.

Mandarin/banded: This circular style was all the rage in the late nineties, and looks nice if you're skipping a tie.

TIES

Bow tie: If you want a classic, conservative look on your wedding day, one that will stand the test of time, embrace the bow tie. Many grooms feel that a clip-on is grossly inappropriate for the wedding day, but be warned: Learning to tie a real bow tie is more difficult than mastering quantum physics. And honestly, no one can tell you're wearing a clip-on anyway.

Four-in-hand ties: If you're a sworn enemy of bow ties, believing they should be worn exclusively by English barristers, rejoice. In recent years, it's become fashionable to wear a four-in-hand tie—the hanging sort you wear with a business suit—with a tuxedo jacket (though never with a shawl lapel). Don't use one you ordinarily wear to work; a tux deserves a splurge.

How to Tie a Bow Tie

The best way to learn to tie a bow tie is to get a salesperson in the formalwear shop you're using to demonstrate. Try it out in front of him. Practice, practice, practice. Then practice some more. In case you need a little extra assistance, follow these instructions.

1. Place the bow tie around your neck, with one end (A) longer than the other (B).

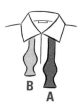

2. Cross longer end A over B.

3. Loop A under the point at which A and B cross.

4. Fold B over itself to form the front base loop of the tie.

5. Fold A over B so that A is oriented straight up and down.

6. Holding everything else in place with one hand, use your other to double the lower portion of A back on itself and poke the newly formed folded edge through the loop behind the tie.

7. Adjust the tie by tugging at the ends (as though dealing with a shoelace) and straightening the center knot until the sides are even.

8. Collapse, sobbing, in a heap (not pictured). Keep practicing, or give up and go with a clip-on.

Wrapping Your Waist

Like Coke vs. Pepsi, the Beatles vs. the Stones, Britney vs. Christina, it's an age-old battle: the cummerbund vs. the waistcoat. You can't have both.

Cummerbund: Believe it or not, that bizarre pleated sash you fasten around your waist like a freakishly large belt once served an actual purpose: The pleats held theater tickets or money. The pleats should always be worn facing up, and the color should match your tie. Add suspenders for a more distinctive look.

Waistcoat: This garment has gotten much more popular in recent years and is generally considered more elegant than a cummerbund. Waistcoats come in an infinite array of patterns, fabrics, and colors and can be an elegant way to add personality to your look— and set yourself apart from the guests and groomsmen. An added plus: It looks great if you want to ditch your jacket when you hit the dance floor. If you're wearing a morning coat or white tie, the waistcoat is the only option for you.

Other Formal Fixin's

Ascot: This broad neck scarf secured with a stickpin can look extremely elegant if your name is Thurston and you're descended from British royalty. Otherwise, it should be reserved for a very formal daytime wedding, when you can pair it with a morning coat.

Cuff links: You've got two options when it comes to these accessories: Keep them simple and match your shirt studs, or use them to express a dash of personality (with smiley faces, say, or the Union Jack).

Boutonniere: Worn on the left lapel of your jacket, this small flower adds a colorful accent to your ensemble. It should match your bride's bouquet, so she should be involved in the selection.

Pocket square: As an alternative to a boutonniere (don't wear both), you can fold this colorful cloth and tuck it into your jacket's left breast pocket. There are an alarming number of folding techniques; the simplest is to fold the cloth into a square so that only the top strip shows.

Dress shoes: With formal attire, low-cut black slip-on shoes or black patent leather dress shoes are traditionally worn. With a suit, patent leather or polished calf dress shoes should suffice. Don't dig a pair out of the closet on the morning of your wedding; either buy new ones or make sure your old ones are shined so they look new.

Socks: They should match the color of your pants. As opposed to everything else you're wearing, the idea is that people shouldn't notice them.

DRESSING DON'TS

* Don't wear something because you just read that it's the next big thing. This is a wedding, not a fashion show. When in doubt, classic and simple should always trump trendy. You don't want your bride to hide your wedding photos out of embarrassment years down the road.

* Don't surprise your bride with your choice of attire. Sure, you're the one wearing the ensemble, but—as in all matters relating to style—your bride knows better than you. And the formality of your ensemble will need to match hers. You don't have to drag her from store to store while you try on everything in sight, but get some guidelines before you go shopping—and make sure she sees your final selection before you put any money down.

* Don't order from a catalog or the Internet. Even if you know your measurements and like the way a tux looks in a photo, you may change your mind once you try it on.

* Don't wait until the last minute. Whether you're buying or renting, you should place an order at least three or four months before your wedding.

* Don't pick up your tux or suit on the day of your wedding. If you're renting, get it *at least* a couple of days in advance so any final problems can be corrected. If you're buying, you should pick up your ensemble a few weeks before the wedding. In either case, ask for a final fitting with the tailor in front of your fiancée or best man.

To Rent or to Buy?

You're getting married. This means it's time to accept that you're a grown-up. Grown-ups own tuxedos. If you've decided on an ensemble you can't ever imagine wearing again—tails, ascot, and top hat, for example—don't shell out the money to buy it. (A good formal-wear store should supply everything you might need to rent, including the accessories.) But if you're wearing a classic black tux, it belongs in your closet after the wedding. You'll need it for the countless weddings you'll have to trudge to over the course of your lifetime—not to mention all those swank black-tie bashes you hope to be invited to someday when you're famous.

If you already own a tux and haven't worn it in a while, don't assume you'll just be able to throw it on the day of your wedding. Get it out of the closet as soon as possible, and make sure it still fits; then be sure to get it cleaned and pressed before the big day so the mold and cobwebs come off.

Get Fit

So, how do you know the tux fits correctly? First of all, only buy or rent from a store that has an on-site tailor who will take all of your measurements before you order the attire and can make any last-minute alterations. And when you pick up your tux, whether you're renting or buying, try it on—every piece of it—to make sure there are no outstanding issues. Here are some general guidelines to follow when it comes to attaining the proper fit.

* Your pants should touch the tops of your shoes.

* Your jacket sleeve should end at your wrist and should allow about half an inch of shirt to show.

* Your shirt collar should not cut off circulation to your head, though it should fit snugly around your neck.

* The bottom of your waistcoat (if you'll be wearing one) should cover the waistband of your trousers.

MONEY-SAVING TIPS: WEDDING ATTIRE

* Forget designer duds. You'll pay extra for a big name.

* Opt for simple styles and basic black. Wearing tails or a fancy patterned vest will add to the cost.

* Check your closet. Before you buy or rent shoes, make sure you don't already have a pair that will work—with a shining.

* Note that some stores will offer deals on groomsmen's ensembles if you're buying or renting your tux there, so be sure to help your pals out by inquiring.

Questions to Ask: Formalwear Hunting

If renting:

* How far ahead of time do I need to reserve the ensemble?

* When would I be able to pick it up?

* What styles of formalwear do you have?

* How old is your inventory?

* Would I be able to see the actual ensemble that you'd be renting to me ahead of time?

* How much is the fee to rent what I'm interested in?

* What parts of the ensemble are included in that cost?

* What is the procedure for alterations? Are they included in the fee? If they're extra, what's the charge?

* Can I have a final fitting in the store, and will someone be available on the spot to make any final alterations? *If the answer is no, go elsewhere.*

* Will the clothes be cleaned and pressed before I receive them?

* When must I return everything?

* What are the late penalties?

* Is there a fee if the ensemble is returned with any stains?

* What is the deposit amount?

* When does the balance need to be paid?

* What is the policy for cancellation?

* Is there a special rate for my groomsmen if I rent my ensemble here?

If buying:

* How far ahead of time would I need to order a tux/suit?

* How does the fitting process work?

* Are alterations included in the price of the tux/suit? If not, what is the fee?

* When it's time for me to pick up the tux/suit, do you provide a final fitting in the store, and is someone available then to make final alterations? *Again, you should not accept no for an answer on this one.*

* When would everything be available for pickup?

* Do you offer rentals for groomsmen? Do you offer discounts on those rentals if I buy my attire here?

* What's the price of the ensemble I'm interested in?

* How much of a deposit do you require?

* When does the balance need to be paid?

* Does the shop carry insurance, and if so, what does that insurance cover?

* What is the policy for canceling an order?

THE WRITTEN WORD: RENTED FORMALWEAR

It is advisable that contracts for rented attire include, but not necessarily be limited to, the following:

* Designer/manufacturer, style number, style, and color of every item you're renting

* List of all accessories you're renting

* Size of every item you're renting

* Account of all services the shop shall perform, including fittings/alterations, cleaning, and pressing

* All fees for attire, accessories, and services, including any discounts

* Date that everything you're renting will be available for pickup

* Shop's policy regarding the return of rented attire, including timing, condition of the attire, and any corresponding penalty fees

* Complete payment schedule and amounts

* Cancellation/refund policy

DRESS TO IMPRESS—LESS: THE GROOMSMEN

Your groomsmen should all be dressed exactly alike, which means, ideally, they should rent formalwear from the same store. The most practical way to do this if you have guys coming from out of town is for them to get measured by a professional tailor and then send you the measurements so you can order their outfits. If you're renting from a formalwear chain, ask out-of-town groomsmen to try on the specific style number you've selected at a branch close to them to ensure the best fit (all ensembles, however, should still be ordered from the same individual shop so as to ensure the best color match).

Note that allowing your groomsmen to do their own ordering from wherever they choose is not advisable. Colors won't match, and there are bound to be differences in the overall look. Even if you don't care, there's a good chance your bride will.

You want your groomsmen to look good—but not quite as good as you. While their attire should match the formality of yours, it is a good idea to set yourself apart in some way. Here are some simple suggestions for achieving this goal.

* If you're going to be wearing a tux with a vest, put your grooms-men in tuxes that match yours, but have them don cummerbunds instead.

* Let your groomsmen wear the same outfit as you, but choose a more colorful or complex boutonniere for yourself.

* Wear a bow tie, but have your groomsmen wear four-in-hand ties.

* Put the groomsmen in ties or vests that match the color of the bridesmaid dresses, while you stick to black, white, or silver.

Chapter Six

The Fun Stuff
The Honeymoon

At this point, you may never want to see a tie or cummerbund again. Relax. Close your eyes. Picture yourself dressed very casually—in a bathing suit, lying on a beach, sipping a rum punch. Lying beside you, a piña colada in her hand, is your bride. In a bikini. A very revealing bikini.

Believe it or not, part of your responsibility as the groom is to ensure that this vision—or some version of it—becomes reality. See, this wedding planning stuff does have its perks. Of course, if you wind up booking a beachside resort in the middle of hurricane season and you have to huddle in an underground shelter for two weeks, you will get all of the blame. So you have to plan carefully, and well in advance, to make your honeymoon as memorable as possible—in a good way.

Honeymoon Planner Timeline

The following planner was designed as a general guide to help you budget your time. That said, the earlier you make your reservations, the better chance you'll have of getting what you want. Flights to and hotels in popular destinations during peak season often book up quickly.

Six to Nine Months Before

☐ Brainstorm with your bride on possible destinations

☐ Get recommendations from friends and relatives for a travel agent, if desired

☐ Talk to recommended travel agents to find the one who's right for you

☐ If you're making the arrangements yourself, start researching destinations, accommodations, and transportation

☐ Make arrangements at your workplace to take time off for the wedding and honeymoon

☐ Check that you and your bride have current passports, or obtain passports if necessary

☐ Acquire any other necessary travel documents, and find out if any vaccinations are required for travel to your destination

☐ Reserve a room for your wedding night

Four to Six Months Before

- ☐ Book a flight or other transportation to your destination
- ☐ Book a place to stay
- ☐ Reserve a rental car, if desired
- ☐ Purchase travel insurance, if desired
- ☐ Research specific activities that you might want to take part in at your destination

Two to Four Months Before

- ☐ Arrange for transportation to airport/station at point of origin and from airport/station at destination, as well as corresponding transportation for the return trip
- ☐ Make arrangements for any specific activities you'll be doing (book day-trip tour, buy theater tickets, etc.)
- ☐ Start making restaurant reservations (many places won't accept reservations until a month in advance, but it's a good idea to call early just in case)
- ☐ Obtain CDs to learn language spoken in honeymoon destination, if applicable

Two Weeks Before

- ☐ Make any necessary arrangements for pets, plants, and house sitter during your absence
- ☐ Purchase traveler's checks, and/or exchange currency

One Week Before

- ☐ Purchase any last-minute items needed for the trip
- ☐ Confirm all reservations for the wedding night room, honeymoon hotel, and transportation
- ☐ Check the weather (a day or two before departure), and pack appropriately

☐ Contact post office to have mail held while you're away

☐ Direct stores where you've registered to hold deliveries

☐ Put a halt to newspaper delivery for the time period that you'll be away

THE WEDDING NIGHT

Before you book that flight to Hawaii, you need to figure out where you'll stay on the night of your wedding. Whether you're tying the knot in an unfamiliar town or just down the street from your house, you should find someplace special to spend your first night as husband and wife. Here are some ideas for setting the stage.

* Find a swank hotel suite or a charming bed-and-breakfast, which will automatically make the wedding night feel like the beginning of your honeymoon. If you're having the wedding at a hotel, ask whomever you've been dealing with about getting a honeymoon suite for the night. Many places will charge only the cost of a regular room, or even include a suite, as part of the wedding package.

* Wherever you wind up staying, make it a tad more romantic by arranging for fresh flowers and a bottle of bubbly. Ask the concierge to help out, and encourage him/her to make some suggestions.

* As a practical matter, you might plan to have some food delivered, since many couples manage to make it through their weddings without finding time to eat. The last thing you want is to pass out from hunger.

* Unless you want to slip back into your sweaty tux the next day, make sure you pack a change of clothes and toiletries (and remind your bride to do the same). Either drop them off at your wedding night spot ahead of time or leave them with the coat check during the wedding and grab them on the way out.

* If you want to stay at home on your wedding night, you can still make it romantic. You'll have to be your own concierge—or enlist the help of some close friends. Have fresh flowers, chilled champagne, and a rose petal–covered bed waiting for you and your new wife. Put on her favorite music, and light some candles when you arrive. And don't forget to carry her over the threshold.

OH, THE PLACES YOU'LL GO

Your first step in honeymoon planning is to narrow down the seemingly infinite list of destinations. By this point, you should realize that rule number one is to consult your bride. Don't pick a place without making sure she's thrilled with it, too. You may have radically different ideas of an ideal honeymoon, so don't assume she wants to lie on a beach all week just because you do. Here are some questions to ask yourselves to help you hone in on your honeymoon spot.

Do we want to be beach bums? If you want to lie around and do absolutely nothing, the beach is the place. Many couples who are looking to relax after several harried months of wedding planning choose this option. Destinations abound, from the Caribbean to Hawaii to Bali. Be sure to find out what the weather is like during the time of year you'd be there—you don't want to arrive only to find out that it's hurricane season.

Are culture and fine dining our priorities? If you're looking for the finest museums and restaurants in the world, consider New York, London, Paris, Rome, Hong Kong, San Francisco, Sydney....

The list goes on and on. And areas such as Provence and Tuscany provide plenty of culture and culinary delights—without the whir of city life. The only drawback is that if you pack in too much sight-seeing, you may return feeling like you need a vacation.

Do we want an exotic experience? If you would prefer a place where you're unlikely to be surrounded by other Americans, go east. Vietnam, Thailand, and India are eager to welcome American tourists. And these places can be inexpensive to boot (once you get there).

Do we want to be social? If you want to schmooze with other couples, consider a cruise. Be forewarned, however, if you get sick of your fellow travelers, it can be tough to avoid them when you're all on a boat together. You'll also want to make sure the cruise attracts people of all ages, since some tend to be popular among retirees. Note, too, that if you're prone to motion sickness, your honeymoon's probably not the best time to test out your sea legs.

Do we want to gamble? You spent a fortune on your wedding—and now you want to win it back at a casino. You're an idiot. That said, if you want to gamble for fun and not for profit, Las Vegas is an obvious possibility, and it's an astounding dining destination as well, offering loads of culinary options. There's also Atlantic City, Monaco, the Bahamas, the Nevada side of Lake Tahoe, Foxwoods and Mohegan Sun in Connecticut, and a growing number of casinos across the United States.

Do we want to party? Every major city has a bar and club scene. If you want something truly raucous, New Orleans and Las Vegas are twenty-four-hour drink fests. If you want to imbibe in a more civilized fashion, try a romantic stay in wine country—perhaps Napa or Sonoma in California, the Burgundy or Bordeaux region of France, or the Rhine Valley in Germany.

Do we want to be pampered? Spas aren't just for women anymore (think couples massage). Options abound all over the United States and abroad—just make sure that any you're considering are geared toward women and men.

Do we want to chill out—literally? If your idea of romance is hitting the ski slopes and then curling up by a fire, you've got a range of options relatively close to home: Aspen or Vail; Killington, Vermont; Park City, Utah; and many more. Or, for a real getaway, consider the Swiss or Austrian Alps.

Do we want to minimize the effort? There's a lot to plan on a honeymoon—where to eat, what to do, how to get around. The logistics are minimized if you're on a cruise or at an all-inclusive resort, where the point is never to leave the premises. Another bonus of an all-inclusive is that you're not constantly pulling out your wallet and being confronted with the amount of money you're spending.

Are we inexplicably drawn to kitsch? If you can tolerate long lines and wailing children, Disney World has got your name all over it. Graceland is Disney World for Elvis fanatics. And there's always the Poconos or Niagara Falls.

Do we want to commune with nature? A honeymoon is often luxurious, but it doesn't have to be. Spending a week or two hiking and camping may be exactly what you and your bride have dreamed of. Check out camping options in Yosemite or Yellowstone, go hiking in Montana's Glacier National Park or Utah's Bryce Canyon, or explore the rain forest in Costa Rica. Hardier (or foolhardier) types might consider an adventure tour, which can take you rock climbing in Tibet or tornado chasing in Oklahoma.

Do we want to be underwater? If both of you are scuba or snorkeling enthusiasts, Australia's Great Barrier Reef can't be beat.

Shorter jaunts can take you to the Cayman Islands and a host of other great diving spots throughout Mexico, the Caribbean, and Hawaii.

How much time do we have? Couples often take off more time for their honeymoons than for typical vacations. Take advantage of this special occasion, and go someplace you couldn't go in a mere week, such as Australia, New Zealand, or Africa.

What's the weather like? Strolling along the Seine in Paris isn't so romantic if you're fighting off frostbite. Don't pick a honeymoon spot without checking to see what the weather will be like when you're actually there.

Are we being safe? Even if danger thrills you, your honeymoon probably isn't the right time to check out an area that's filled with political unrest. For an up-to-date list of the U.S. government's travel warnings and advisories, check out www.travel.state.gov.

What will we do when we get there? Once you narrow down your list of options, you and your bride should continue to ask yourselves what will make you happy honeymooners. Do you want to golf? Play tennis? Shop? Check out guidebooks and brochures or consult with your travel agent, and find a place that can satisfy your most important requirements.

 Guru Grooms on...

Getting Away

"I was working at a job where the bosses were suspicious if people took long vacations—so no one ever did. But your honeymoon is the one time nobody questions it, so it was a good chance to go somewhere far away. We went to Hawaii and had a great time."

—*Eric, 31, New York*

Honeymoon Harmony

If you both want the same thing on your honeymoon, you're in luck. But what happens when you want to lie on the beach and your bride wishes to museum-hop? Here are a few ways to deal when you disagree.

Split the trip in two. Treat your honeymoon as two minivacations—one to a city and one to a beach, or one to a spa and one to a hiking destination. This is easier than it sounds; often enough, a beach resort town is a short drive or train ride from a major city, and numerous spas have found homes in areas where you can commune with nature (many, in fact, offer hiking excursions).

Find the right spot. She wants culture, and you want to sunbathe? Check out the French Riviera, Spain's Costa del Sol, or good ol' Miami, to name just a few possible destinations. Spend a few days doing her thing and a few doing yours.

Give her this one—and give yourself the next. Sure, it's your honeymoon, but it's not the last vacation you'll ever take (unless kids are on the way). So let her have her way, but agree that the next time you travel, you get to do what you want.

Money-Saving Tips: Honeymoon Planning

* Travel off-season. A gorgeous resort in the Caribbean, for instance, can be stunningly expensive in February and a relative steal in July. Just make sure that you've investigated the weather conditions and are comfortable with them; there's a reason certain times of year are cheaper than others.

* Consider an all-inclusive resort. If you're worried about going over budget, such a place can keep you in line. Always check the fine print, but in most cases, you pay one price up front that covers everything—all food, booze (though this varies from place to

place), basic water sports, even gratuities. But beware: Some resorts are aimed at families (read: screaming children abound), others at couples, and others at singles. Do your research.

* Book your trip far in advance. Resorts and cruises often offer discounts to people who make reservations more than six months ahead of time.

* Use the Internet—wisely. For hotel deals, try www.quikbook.com and www.hotels.com. For flights, try www.orbitz.com and www.cheaptickets.com. And don't forget to check out such giants as expedia.com and travelocity.com.

* Forget the far-off trip. The farther you fly, the higher the cost.

* Check your frequent flier accounts to see if you and your bride have enough miles to get you where you want to go. (If you're shelling out actual dollars for the trip, be sure to provide the airline with your frequent flier numbers—or join the program if you don't already belong—so you can both rack up miles.)

* When booking a flight, find out if there's a different route that's cheaper. Sometimes an itinerary that entails changing planes costs less than a nonstop flight. That said, it is your honeymoon; think about whether the added hassle is worth it.

* Check alternate airports. Flying into or out of a smaller airport—Oakland instead of San Francisco, or Islip, Long Island, instead of LaGuardia, for instance—can save you bucks on airfare.

Going-Away Present

Consider registering for your honeymoon. Many travel agencies and online travel services enable you to set up a bridal registry so wedding guests can contribute money toward your honeymoon as their gift to you.

* Play the honeymoon card. Tell anyone and everyone that you're newlyweds on your honeymoon—when you're making any kind of reservation, when you arrive, and whenever else you can. It might get you squat—or it might get you upgrades, free bottles of champagne, and all-around better service.

* If you're traveling to a foreign country, don't exchange currency at hotels, which tend to charge higher fees. Use your ATM card or change money at a bank, or charge expenses to your credit card, which often gets you the best exchange rate.

* Beware the extra fees. Avoid making calls from your hotel phone, and never, ever touch the minibar. Check your hotel bill very carefully to make sure you haven't been wrongly charged for an $8 bag of potato chips.

* Return any rental car with a full tank of gas. Rental companies charge an absurd amount per gallon if they have to fill up the tank.

The Dos and Don'ts of Honeymoon Planning

Dos

* Set a budget. Before you begin planning, figure out what you can really afford to spend overall.

* Think about going through a travel agent. You may never have used one before, but this is one time when having an expert on your side could be worth it.

* Consider how long it takes to travel to a potential destination. If one of you hates flying, a twelve-hour airplane ride may not be the best way to begin married life.

* Consider leaving two days after your wedding instead of immediately after the reception or the next day. That way, on your wedding night, you won't be thinking about how you've got to

get up at five o'clock the next morning to make your flight. Plus, giving yourself an extra day allows you to have a leisurely morning with your new wife and to hit the store for any last-minute items you need for your trip.

* Look at some photos of the property and rooms comparable to what you'd be reserving before booking a hotel room (and show them to your bride as well). Many hotels have websites featuring such images; you can also request brochures. If you—or, more to the point, your bride—has certain expectations and the accommodations are drastically different, there could be disappointment (to say the least) down the road.

* Use your bride's maiden name when booking her airline tickets, even if she's taking your last name. The name on her ticket should match her passport, her driver's license, and any other travel documents. To ensure maximum comfort, request an aisle or window seat—whichever you prefer.

* Determine whether your car insurance covers you on a rental car in the area(s) you'll be driving before you buy insurance through the rental agency.

* Find out the policies for payment, reservation changes, and cancellation when making arrangements for accommodations and transportation—before putting money down.

* Get a confirmation number for every reservation you make.

* Consider purchasing travel insurance. Policies vary, but they can protect you if you need to cancel your honeymoon because of illness or an emergency; some also cover theft during the trip. (Some companies offer policies that cover acts of terrorism as well.) Coverage can be purchased through a travel agency or an insurance company. Make sure, however, that you're not

already covered by your homeowner's or renter's insurance or through your credit card company.

Don'ts

* Don't be afraid to splurge. This is your honeymoon, after all. You shouldn't spend beyond your means, but this isn't the time to cut corners either.

* Don't go back to work the day after your wedding, even if you're delaying the big honeymoon. Take a couples of days off for a quick getaway—or even to lounge around the house together. You've just been through a lot. You can use the time off.

* Don't go someplace you've been with an ex. If you and a former girlfriend went to the most romantic bed-and-breakfast in the world, sorry. You can't go back—not on your honeymoon.

* Don't be unprepared. If you're going abroad, learn a little of the language—at a minimum, you should be able to ask directions, order food in a restaurant, and say "hello," "please," "thank you," and "excuse me." You should also research your destination via guidebooks or the Internet.

* Don't run yourself ragged. Even if you're heading to a big city, give yourself a day or two to relax and recuperate from your wedding before you start your sightseeing sprint.

How to Choose a Travel Agent

If you've never used a travel agent before, you shouldn't be afraid to start now. This approach takes some of the planning pressure off you, and a travel agent is likely to have a long list of places that have satisfied honeymooners in the past.

To find a travel agent, ask for recommendations from family and friends. Talk to people who have recently been married, and ask whom they used to help plan their honeymoons. Or check the website of the American Society of Travel Agents at www.astanet.com for a list of local recommendations. Once you've gotten some names, shop around to find the right person for you. Below are some questions to ask when meeting with prospective travel agents. And before you book a trip, see Do Your Homework, which starts on page 100.

* Is there a particular type of trip or a certain geographic area that you specialize in?

* How many years has your agency been in business?

* What's included in your services?

* Do you have any specific suggestions or advice regarding places we should go?

* Have you been to the specific places you're suggesting? *It's best if a travel agent has firsthand knowledge of your destination and isn't just gathering info from promotional materials—something you could do yourself.*

* Do you have photos showing the grounds and the interiors of typical rooms of the hotels we're considering?

* Can you give us references and contact information for other couples who have booked their honeymoons through your

agency? *Before selecting a travel agent, you should check with at least three other couples who used his/her services for a similar honeymoon.*

* How much does the trip we're considering cost, and what, exactly, is included in that amount?

* Will you deliver all of the tickets, confirmations, maps, and brochures we need, or do we need to pick them up?

* Will you help us get any other travel documents we need, such as passports and visas?

* What kind of travel insurance can we obtain through you? What exactly does it cover, and what's the cost?

* What is the payment policy?

* What's the cancellation policy?

* Is there a twenty-four-hour toll-free emergency number where we can reach someone from your agency in case of a problem on our trip? *If you show up at a hotel or train station to find that there's no record of your reservation, you want to be able to call your travel agency and have someone there fix the problem at any time, day or night.*

Do Your Homework: Questions to Ask When Making Travel Arrangements

Regardless of whether you're going through a travel agent or making reservations on your own, take into account the considerations detailed below. While no honeymoon may be perfect, you can certainly minimize any headaches and heartache by planning ahead and asking the right questions up front.

Home Away from Home: Hotel Accommodations

* Can we get a room with a view (ocean, garden, etc.)? *Find out what your options are. Looking onto a parking lot is not romantic; neither is facing a noisy street with heavy traffic.*

* What amenities are included in the room (fireplace, whirlpool tub, television, radio, refrigerator, etc.)?

* Does the room have a private bath? *If you're staying at a quaint B&B, for instance, you may be sharing with other guests, so be sure to inquire.*

* What amenities does the hotel property feature (swimming pool, hot tub, gym, spa, tennis courts, restaurant, etc.)?

* What is the rate for the room?

* What is included in that rate?

* Is room service offered?

* Is there shuttle service between the hotel and the airport? If so, is it complimentary or is there a fee?

* Do you rent out sports gear (bicycles, rackets, scuba equipment, skis, etc.)? If not, can you suggest a place that does?

* Is the room air-conditioned? *If you're staying at a hotel in warm weather and a fan doesn't cut it for you, this could be a key factor in your decision.*

Happiness on the High Seas: Cruise Considerations

* What are our options for accommodations? How do they differ in terms of size, view, amenities, and price?

* What amenities does the ship feature?

* What kinds of activities and entertainment are offered?

* How much time will we get to spend in each port of call? Does the cruise offer any tours at these stops?

Attitude Is Everything:
The Secret to a Successful Honeymoon

While you can certainly take steps to minimize problems, there are obviously things that lie beyond your control. Freak rainstorms could hit during a usually clear time of year. Your luggage could get lost. While couples—brides especially—want the honeymoon to be perfect, you are still living in the real world, where things do go wrong on occasion. But what will make or break the trip is how you react to any hurdles that present themselves. And know that the way *you* cope will affect how your bride copes. If you try laughing at mishaps, those mishaps will start to seem truly minor, and you'll have a wonderful time despite them. Unless you get food poisoning. In that case, you're screwed.

* Do we need a passport or any other travel documents?

* What exactly is included in the cruise fare, and what "extras" will we need to pay for?

* Are meals included? What about port charges and taxes?

* Is there a dress code?

* Does this particular cruise attract a certain age group?

TRAVEL TIPS

* Check the weather a day or two before you leave. If a heat wave or cold snap is on the way, you'll want to pack appropriately rather than spend your first day of the trip buying clothes.

* If you're taking traveler's checks with you, copy down the numbers of the checks and keep this piece of paper in a separate place; that way, if the checks get lost or stolen, you'll have a record.

* Pack a carry-on bag with toiletries, a toothbrush and toothpaste, any necessary medication, and a change of clothes. If your luggage doesn't arrive for a day or two, you'll be covered.

Chapter Seven

The Pressure's On
The Rehearsal Dinner (and Other Activities)

If you're sticking with the traditional breakdown of duties, all you really have to do when it comes to the wedding reception is show up. The party to end all parties, the reception is your bride's time to shine. Your big night is the reception's Mini-Me: the rehearsal dinner, generally held the night before the wedding.

First, of course, comes the rehearsal itself. Everyone involved in the actual wedding ceremony should gather—officiant included—to go over his/her role and participate in a brief run-through. The entire rehearsal can last anywhere from ten minutes to an hour.

After this bit of business has been taken care of, the fun begins with the rehearsal dinner. Traditionally, this event is hosted by the parents of the groom, though today it's sometimes hosted by the happy couple themselves or by parents on both sides. Even if your parents are throwing this bash, you shouldn't let them plan the whole thing (though by all means, if they offer, let them *pay* for the whole thing). The following checklist provides an overview of what's involved in pulling this party off.

Things to Do: The Rehearsal Dinner

☐ Talk to your parents about what type of event to throw; figure out a budget and who will be paying

☐ Start working on the guest list with your bride (as with the wedding, each party involved gets a portion of the list)

☐ Choose a location, and reserve it

☐ Book a caterer, if applicable

☐ Figure out the menu, and decide what sort of bar setup you'll have

☐ Collect all contact information necessary for inviting guests

☐ Make arrangements for any desired decorations (flowers, candles, etc.)

☐ Arrange for any desired background music

☐ Make arrangements for any desired entertainment or activities (see page 113)

☐ Finalize the guest list

☐ Extend invitations

☐ Write a toast (with your bride)

☐ Follow up with invitees who have not responded by the designated date

☐ Provide the site manager with the final head count

☐ Give the caterer the final head count

☐ Confirm all arrangements with the site manager

☐ Confirm all details with the caterer

GENERAL GUIDELINES

* Your rehearsal dinner should be less formal than your wedding reception. Overall, this prewedding event is more relaxed in tone—it's a time to have fun, not worry about which fork to use. Plus, you don't want guests reminiscing, "Yeah, the wedding was nice, but that rehearsal dinner—now that was something really special." When you're picking a place, don't outdo the reception site.

* To make life easier on yourself, select a venue that's relatively close to the rehearsal site, since that's most likely where you'll be coming from.

* Work with your bride on the timing. You don't want guests arriving at the rehearsal dinner while the wedding party is still practicing walking down the aisle—miles away.

* Your menu should be substantially different from that of the wedding reception. No one wants to eat the same type of food two nights in a row.

NOT ANOTHER GUEST LIST

Yes, you've got to go through this process yet again. This instance, however, should be less agonizing since you've already got a basic starting point. It's just a question of who makes the cut from the wedding list.

* The mandatory guests are as follows: the bride and groom, their parents and siblings, grandparents, the members of the wedding party, special ceremony participants (such as anyone you've chosen to give a reading), and the officiant if he/she has been invited to the wedding reception; significant others of these invitees should be included as well. You should also invite the parents of the following: flower girl, ring bearer, and any other kids who are involved in the wedding ceremony. As for the kids themselves, unless you've set a strict no-children policy for your dinner, they should be invited too.

* You might also wish to invite close friends and family members you couldn't include in your wedding party—the ones whose egos you crushed. Now is your opportunity to make it up to them—and assuage your own guilt—by officially letting them know that they make the close-friend cut.

* Others you may want to invite include aunts and uncles. You might consider including first cousins as well.

* Last but not least, many hosts invite those wedding guests who have traveled from afar. While you're certainly not required to do this, it's a nice gesture for people who have made a substantial effort to watch you enter wedded bliss.

* When deciding where to draw the line, keep in mind not only the obvious budgetary factors, but also the tone that you're trying to achieve; the smaller the guest list, the more intimate a gathering you'll have.

Party Pointer

When deciding upon a place for the rehearsal dinner, make sure you have plenty of privacy: You should have a private room or be comfortably separated from other patrons. This is a time to let it all hang out, have fun, and give toasts—you don't want to worry about disturbing other diners or having other diners interfere with your party.

PICKING THE PLACE: INSPIRING IDEAS

* Reserve a private room at a favorite local restaurant—or in the restaurant at a hotel where many wedding guests are staying.

* Ask the concierge at the hotel where most guests are staying if you can set up a private dinner somewhere less conventional— around the pool or garden, for example (be sure to inquire how much privacy you'll have, though).

* Think ethnic. Weddings often serve formal, frenchified fare, so hold your rehearsal dinner at a casual pan–Latin American or upscale Asian spot.

* Try a casual buffet at a local country club.

* Host a clambake on the beach.

* If your parents can endure the added stress, host the dinner at their place.

* Have a barbecue in your parents' backyard or a rented outdoor space (just be sure to have a backup plan in case Mother Nature doesn't cooperate).

* Put together a picnic in a local park or at a vineyard.

* Return to the scene of the crime—the place where you and the bride went on your first date. Your guests will be touched (or amused, anyway) by the sentiment.

MONEY-SAVING TIPS: THE REHEARSAL DINNER

Keep it casual. A barbecue will be cheaper—and, often, more fun—than a sit-down dinner at a chic restaurant.

Keep it small. Limit the guest list to mandatory invitees (turn back to page 106 for an account of whom you must invite).

Keep the invites low-rent. You don't have to have invitations made up for the occasion, and you certainly don't need a calligrapher. Buy preprinted cards and simply fill in the details, or make your own invites on a computer. Inviting guests by e-mail is a sure way to save some dough.

Ditch the flowers. Accent tables with greenery or candles.

Ditch the waiters. Buffets are usually cheaper than a seated meal, since there are fewer wait staff members to pay.

Ditch the full bar. Serve only wine and beer to keep the tab down.

Make it early. Have the actual rehearsal earlier in the afternoon so that the post-rehearsal gathering can be a cocktail party (beverages and finger foods only). Just make sure you specify "cocktail reception" on the invitation so everyone knows to make plans for dinner.

Bring your own booze. This approach can be less expensive than letting the site or caterer provide the alcohol. Just be sure to ask if there's a corkage fee (a sum charged by the site or caterer for opening bottles that you bring in), and factor that amount into your calculations.

Questions to Ask: Site Manager

Following are some questions to ask before booking a venue for the rehearsal dinner. Those questions that appear in italics should be asked of a caterer, if you'll be hiring one. Be sure to inquire whether the caterer provides wait staff as well. For more questions specific to caterers, see page 111. And note that if you're looking at a venue that's basically a hall, as opposed to a restaurant, you'll need to find out what's provided in terms of tables, plates, glasses, flatware, napkins, tablecloths, etc., as well as whether you can bring in an outside caterer and whether or not the site has kitchen facilities.

* What is the capacity of the space?

* *Do we need to guarantee a minimum number of guests to use the facility?*

* How much privacy will we have?

* Will there be other events while we're having ours?

* *Do we have the option of a seated meal or a buffet?*

* *What are our menu options?*

* *How do you handle special dietary requests?*

* Will we have a maître d' devoted only to our party?

* Will there be wait staff serving only our party? *You should insist on having wait staff devoted solely to your event to ensure that your party's needs are addressed in a timely fashion.*

* *What will the server-to-guest ratio be?*

* How many people can comfortably be accommodated at each table?

* *What is the total fee, and what is included in that amount?*

* *Are tips included?*

* *What are our bar options, and what are the corresponding fees?*

* *What label of alcohol do you serve?*

* *Are we permitted to supply the alcohol? If so, do you charge a corkage fee?*

* For how long would we have the space?

* What happens if we run over the designated time? Is there an overtime fee?

* Before we book, can we see the space set up for a similar type of party?

* Does the facility have valet parking? Does it cost extra? How much?

* Do you have an attended coat room? If so, is there an extra charge for using it?

* Will there be candles or flowers on the tables?

* Can we provide our own decorations, and if so, are there any restrictions?

* Can we bring in music (live or recorded)? What are you equipped for? Are there any restrictions?

* Is the room air-conditioned? *You want to ensure the comfort of your guests if it's a warm-weather month.*

* *What is the deadline for the final head count?*

* Does the venue have liability insurance?

* *How much of a deposit must we put down?*

* *When does the balance need to be paid?*

* *What is the policy for cancellation?*

* *Can you give me the names and contact information of three references who had similar events?*

More Questions to Ask: Caterer

If you'll be working with a caterer, ask those questions that appear in italics in the site manager interview starting on page 109, as well as the following.

* Do you provide tables and chairs? If so, how many people does each table comfortably accommodate?

* Is the venue where we're having the dinner fully equipped for your needs?

* Do you bring all of your cooking equipment, or do we need to supply anything?

* Do you provide tablecloths, napkins, serving dishes, china, flatware, and glasses? Is there anything we need to supply?

* Do you do all of the setting up and cleaning up? How much time before and after the event do you allot for those tasks?

* Are there any overtime fees, and when would they kick in?

* Are there any other fees that haven't been discussed?

* Do you have liability insurance?

Word of Warning

After the rehearsal dinner, your friends will inevitably want to adjourn to a nearby club or bar to catch up. That's fine—for them. They're not getting married the next day. The temptation may be great, but be careful about partying—and drinking—into the wee hours of the morning. Save yourself for the main event (that would be the wedding).

INVITATIONS IN BRIEF

Don't worry—unlike wedding invitations, there are only a few basics to keep in mind.

* Invitations should go out shortly after the wedding invites.

* To facilitate planning (especially if you need to give a site manager or caterer a final head count), give guests a date by which they should RSVP.

* As far in advance as possible, give nonlocal invitees a heads-up about the rehearsal dinner (before the actual invitations are sent); that way out-of-towners have time to make the appropriate travel arrangements.

* Since the rehearsal dinner is more casual than the wedding, the invitations can be more casual too. This means you can invite guests over the phone or via e-mail.

OTHER THINGS TO THINK ABOUT

Seating arrangements: Will you assign seats and use place cards, or let guests choose their dining companions for themselves? On the one hand, friends and family might welcome the opportunity to sit wherever and with whomever they like, especially if there's assigned seating at the wedding. On the other hand, a lack of assigned seating can result in a free-for-all. If you go with designated seats, consider mixing it up a bit—seating some of the bride's family with your own.

Entertainment: No stripteases (save that for the bachelor party). However, it's not unheard-of to present some sort of slide show of you and your bride growing up. It gives your family and friends the opportunity to laugh at your gawky stages and gush over your cute ones. If you go this route, make sure that the site can accommodate your needs.

Gifts: Many couples give their attendants tokens of appreciation at the rehearsal dinner. For a list of ideas, see page 137.

TOASTING TIPS

* It is customary for the bride and groom to give a brief speech thanking all of the guests for coming and for being a part of such a special event.

* Your toast at the rehearsal dinner is also a good opportunity to thank your parents for all of their support and, if applicable, for throwing the dinner or the wedding.

* You and your bride can each say a few words, or one of you can be the designated spokesperson, but the speech should sound like it comes from both of you.

* Whoever shelled out the dough for this shindig is also expected to thank people for coming and might offer a few words expressing joy about the coming nuptials.

* Many other people may wish to raise a glass at your rehearsal dinner, including:

   The best man. He's saddled with the wedding reception speech, so you may want to give him the night off. But if he grooves on this sort of thing, by all means ask him to compose a few words.

   The maid of honor. These days, the maid of honor frequently gives a toast at the wedding reception as well; if she isn't doing so, she traditionally makes a toast at the rehearsal dinner instead. And, like the best man, she can speak at both if that makes her happy.

   Everyone else. As opposed to the carefully choreographed nature of a wedding reception, the rehearsal dinner is meant to be more freewheeling and spontaneous. In other words, anyone who wants to give a toast can do so, and often a few close friends of both the bride and groom will offer some words. If you're hoping for a slew of speeches, let your friends and family know in advance that you'd love for them to give toasts; that way they'll have some time to prepare.

* Toasts at a rehearsal dinner tend to be more humorous or risqué than the sentimental speeches given at a wedding. Silly poems are popular (though if any start with "There once was a man from Nantucket," immediately feign a choking fit and flee the premises).

* Certain topics should definitely be off-limits. Your ex-girlfriends should never, ever be mentioned, nor should anything that will make your grandparents go into cardiac arrest. If you have any

friends who might not know the proper boundaries, have a talk with them. This can be done in a way that isn't horribly insulting. Start by telling your pal that it would mean a lot if he said a few words at the rehearsal dinner. Then mention that your Grandma Ethel believes you've led an existence free of vice and that he should be careful not to shatter her illusions by mentioning that time you were arrested for running a speakeasy out of your basement.

THE WEDDING WEEKEND: KEEPING THE GUESTS OCCUPIED

If they had to travel, the friends and family you're inviting to the wedding may have lots of downtime—and they probably don't want to spend the entire day sitting in a hotel room watching soap operas as they wait for the rehearsal dinner and/or the wedding itself. (If they do, get them help—fast.) You and your bride might want to give them options for passing the time. Here are a few simple suggestions.

* If you're getting married in a major city, you've got it easy. Come up with a list of top museums, movie theaters, boutique stores or unusual shops, and other tourist attractions that will be easy for out-of-towners to get to. Put this list in the mail a few weeks before they arrive, or leave a copy in their hotel rooms. Include detailed directions (via public transportation, car, or foot), addresses, phone numbers, and hours of operation for each attraction. Your guests should be able to take it from there.

* Consider organizing some kind of group activity, such as a soft-ball game, a round-robin tennis tournament, an outing to a bowling alley, or a trip to a miniature golf course.

* Though a chocolate bar and a bag of chips won't really keep your guests busy all weekend, leaving gift baskets in their hotel rooms is a thoughtful gesture. A few snacks and some bottled water, along with a map of the area and a schedule of wedding events, are all you need.

* If the majority of guests are crashing at the same hotel, consider arranging for a hospitality suite—a room where the wedding guests can hang out with one another, grab some food, and kill time. That way they've got some company, but you don't have to baby-sit them.

Block Party

It is customary for couples to arrange for blocks of rooms at nearby hotels to be held for guests at a discounted rate. (Don't worry—the guests pay, not you.) Before making such arrangements, check out the hotels in person to make sure that they're suitable for your friends and relatives (you don't want to send them to a dump, after all). Once the arrangements have been made, send out-of-towners all of the per-tinent information, including the name or code they need to provide in order to receive the discount when making reservations. You can also include information about local attractions in this mailing.

Chapter Eight

The Nitty Gritty

Some of you out there are lucky enough to be detail-oriented (to put it kindly) or anal-retentive (to put it honestly). Most of you, being men, are not. You're disorganized. You're slobs. You're used to overlooking the details—or delegating them to someone else.

In most aspects of life, you can get away with this. Not this time. When it comes to planning a wedding, there are many seemingly minor details that are easy to overlook. If you do overlook them, you'll find out way too late that they weren't minor after all. This chapter covers some of the little things that make the big picture come together.

Moving the Masses: Transportation

You and your bride will need to decide how each of you, your immediate families, and the members of your wedding party will get from place to place on the big day. You might also want to consider how your guests are going to get around.

Things to Do

☐ Make arrangements for yourself, the bride, the wedding party, and immediate family to get to the ceremony and reception

☐ Make arrangements for your transportation after the reception

☐ Arrange for post-reception transportation for immediate family and the wedding party

☐ Send a signed contract and deposit to the transportation company

☐ Hire a shuttle service to take guests to and from the wedding, if desired

☐ Give drivers detailed directions, addresses, and contact numbers

☐ If you're using your own vehicle or borrowing one from a family member, fill up the gas tank

☐ Confirm transportation details

UNDERSTANDING YOUR OPTIONS

When it comes to the wedding party, many couples opt to rent a limo or limos so they can all arrive in style. The advantages are obvious: You don't have to worry about your own car, you don't have to be concerned about drinking and driving, and you look really, really good. The disadvantage: As you're being pronounced husband and wife and partying into the night, you're paying a fortune to have a driver sit in the car and work his way through his CD collection.

If you don't believe in superstition, you can certainly ride along with your wife-to-be to the ceremony site. But if you think that seeing your bride before the moment of your wedding will somehow doom your chances for marital happiness, you can hire multiple cars or have the limo drive your bride and her bridesmaids while you catch a lift with your best man. Once you have made it legal, you can join your wife in the limousine to the reception location. Depending on where you're tying the knot, other options such as a horse and buggy, a gondola ride, or a vintage convertible can add an elegant touch.

As for the other guests, you're certainly not obligated to provide transportation. If the majority of guests are from the area, they've got their own cars and can give out-of-towners rides. And those who flew into town can obviously rent a car for their stay. If you're getting married in a city, guests can catch cabs or walk from nearby hotels. The bottom line is these people are grown-ups—they can take care of themselves.

That said, if you do have a lot of nonlocal guests attending the wedding, it's a nice gesture to hire a van or shuttle bus service to take them to and from the ceremony and reception sites. Many wedding hosts also take this approach in order to minimize the chance of guests drinking and driving.

Booking Basics

If you opt for limos, other types of rental cars, and/or a shuttle service, here are a few steps toward ensuring a smooth ride.

* Book well in advance. Start looking for vehicles six months before your wedding date. That should give you time to shop around and choose the best service. You should sign a contract at least two months before the big day. If your wedding falls near Christmas or prom season, book even further ahead.

* Don't just rely on the phone book. Ask for recommendations from friends and relatives, and check with the Better Business Bureau to make sure the company you're considering is reliable.

* Inspect the vehicles—inside and out. A shiny limo is a shiny limo, right? Sure, until you open the door and find out the upholstery is peeling, the seat belts are broken, the air stinks of cigar smoke, and a dozen high school kids are still inside passed out from prom night. Make sure you see the exact car or bus you'll be riding in. Check, first, that it can fit as many people as you need it to. And verify, in writing, the model and color so that the service cannot pull any last-minute switches. Otherwise, the company may claim your black town car was busy—and leave you with a hot pink number instead. Not that there's anything wrong with that.

* Chat up the chauffeur. Find out who your driver will be and meet him/her in person—far enough in advance that you can request a switch if, say, he curses like a sailor or refers to weddings as "the devil's work."

* Keep it classy. There's a very, very fine line between elegance and tackiness. Renting a limo that fits forty-five people when you're using it for only you and your bride is tacky. Renting an old Rolls Royce: classy.

* Tell the limo or bus to come early. If you want to be picked up at 5:30, let the service know you need to be picked up at 5:00. Yes, it will add to the cost, but this way if the driver hits traffic and shows up fifteen minutes late, you won't panic.

MONEY-SAVING TIPS: TRANSPORTATION

* Can the chauffeur. When it comes to you and your bride, rent a nice car and make one of your groomsmen or close nondrinking friends the designated driver for the night. That way you can still arrive in style but without the expense of a driver.

* Find out what it costs for the driver to wait through the entire reception. Compare that with the cost of renting two cars and drivers—one to take you to the wedding, and another to come pick you up hours later. Hiring two separate cars may be cheaper than paying a driver to sit in a parking lot all night.

* Pay for a fancy arrival or departure—but not both. If you're arriving at the ceremony site for photos hours before the guests arrive, do you really need to pull up in a stretch limo? Consider arranging for a fancy getaway car but just catching a cab or driving with a pal to the ceremony. Likewise, if you're spending the night two blocks away from your reception site, does it really pay to spend thirty-eight seconds riding in luxury?

* Go with a town car instead of a limo.

* Let the wedding party drive themselves so you have fewer cars to worry about.

* Go bare-bones. A car company may have limos that look great on the outside but don't come with a TV or bar on the inside—and are cheaper than the amenities-packed versions.

* If you're getting married in the middle of a big city and the ceremony and reception venues are not too far apart, consider walking between the two. A procession of wedding guests led by the bride and groom can make for a spectacular sight, great photos, and a memorable part of the overall event (provided it's not pouring rain, in which case cabs might be in order).

Questions to Ask: Transportation Service

* What makes, models, and colors do you offer?

* How many people can comfortably ride in each vehicle that we're considering?

* How old are the vehicles?

* Can we inspect the vehicles we'll be using?

* What's the length of employment at your company for each of the drivers who would be assigned to our party?

* What are their driving records?

* Do these drivers know the area well?

* Can we talk to the drivers in person?

* What will the drivers wear?

* Is there a minimum number of hours required for using your service?

* What's the fee for the vehicles and services we're discussing? Are tips included or extra?

* Are there any other charges?

* What special features (bar, TV, etc.) do the vehicles have? Are these included in the price? If not, what is the added cost?

* How many hours does the fee cover?

* Do you have any wedding packages? What's included?

* If we're paying by the hour, are we charged from the time that passengers are picked up or from the time that the driver starts out for his/her first pickup?

* What are we charged if we run over the allotted time?

* Will the drivers wait for us at our venue(s) throughout the entire event? Does that affect the cost?

* Do you have insurance, and if so, what does it cover? *If a service does not carry insurance that covers liability and you and your wedding party in the event of an accident, you should take your business elsewhere.*

* What is the payment policy and schedule?

* What is the cancellation policy?

* Can you give us the names and numbers of some couples who used your service for weddings so we can use them as references?

THE WRITTEN WORD: TRANSPORTATION

It is advisable that contracts include, but not necessarily be limited to, the following.

* Date and times of service

* Addresses of all pickup and drop-off points

* Descriptions of vehicles, including make, model, and color

* How many vehicles (of each type) are being provided

* Detailed account of all amenities

* How many drivers are being provided

* Account of anything else that has been agreed upon, such as the fact that the driver will wait at a certain location during the event if that is part of the deal

* Description of what drivers will be wearing

* All fees, including overtime fees, as well as charges for parking and/or tolls

* Description of the insurance coverage the company carries

* Payment schedule (including amounts) and policy

* Cancellation/refund policy

MAKING IT LEGAL: THE MARRIAGE LICENSE

Getting a license is the least romantic part of wedding planning. At best, you wait in line in some anonymous office, then face a surly clerk whose job it is to suck all the joy out of your day. At worst, you also need to have a needle stuck in your vein at some point. But you've got to take care of this or you won't be legally married. This is the sort of detail your bride will *never* forgive you for forgetting.

Annoyingly enough, requirements for getting a marriage license vary widely across the country. You can't wait until the last second (except in Vegas, where a man dressed as Elvis can legally give you a license *and* perform the ceremony), but if you get a license too early, it may expire. So make sure you contact the local town clerk's office where you're getting married far in advance to find out when you need to get your license and what the requirements are. Be sure to ask the following.

* Where do we need to show up to obtain the marriage license?

* What do we need to bring with us? *It's likely you'll each need to bring two forms of ID; make sure to find out what types of ID are acceptable. If either of you has been married before, you'll probably need to show proof that the previous marriage is legally over; again, find out the specific documents that will be accepted.*

* What is the fee for the license, and what kind of payment is accepted?

* Do we need to get blood tests, and if so, what exactly do we need to be tested for?

* Where can we have these tests done, and what kind of documentation is required?

You may also want to find out when the least busy times are to show up and how long it will take for you to receive your license.

Once you've got your license, it will need to be signed by the officiant and, depending on the requirements, at least one witness on your wedding day, then mailed back to the appropriate government office—either by you or the officiant. At that point, your marriage will be officially recorded and you'll be sent a marriage certificate, which provides proof of your wedded status. If by any chance you don't receive this document within a month or two of your wedding, request it. Once it's in your hands, file it someplace safe.

Band Together: The Wedding Rings

* Once you've gone through the process of buying an engagement ring, getting wedding bands is a snap. For one thing, there's no hunk of shiny rock to worry about. For another, you and your bride are *expected* to go shopping together so you can pick out

matching (or complementary) bands. This means you don't have to worry about buying her a piece of jewelry she secretly despises.

* Most wedding rings are simple bands of gold, white gold, or platinum, though they can have stones embedded in them as well. (If you're having a religious ceremony, ask the officiant whether there are any restrictions regarding your wedding bands.)

* If you're feeling schmaltzy, you can have the wedding date or your names inscribed on the inside of the rings.

* If you've never worn a ring before, yes, it will feel weird at first, but you'll get used to it. Kinda like being married.

Questions to Ask: Ring Shopping

* How long will it take before the rings are ready?

* How much do the rings cost?

* Will it be possible to have the rings resized at a later point if necessary?

* Do you charge an extra fee to resize the rings? *Unless a decorative element prevents this, resizing should be free.*

* Can we have the rings engraved here, and if so, what's the fee? How much time does this add?

* What is the payment policy?

* What is the cancellation policy?

PLEASE BE SEATED

Mapping out the seating arrangements at the reception is a logistical nightmare of trial and error. Unfortunately, no book can make this process any easier. But before you begin figuring out where all of your guests will be situated, you need to decide where you and your lovely bride will sit. It comes down to a simple matter of taste, but there are pluses and minuses to the four most common options.

1. The bride and groom sit with the wedding party at a long rectangular table or a round table.

    Pros: It singles out the members of the wedding party—who are, after all, very important to you.

    Cons: They've already been singled out during the ceremony. And while your best friend is happy to sit with you, his significant other probably isn't thrilled to be sitting at a different table with all of the other better halves. Separating a couple can be less than ideal.

2. The newlyweds sit alone at a small table, known as a sweetheart table (don't let the name dissuade you).

    Pros: It keeps the attention where it belongs—on you. And it prevents you from having to play favorites by choosing tablemates.

    Cons: It's a wedding, not a coronation, but this setup can make guests feel as though they're supposed to bring you sacrificed animals or kiss your feet. Besides, this is a day to share with other people—otherwise you would have eloped (too late now).

3. The bride and groom sit with friends or relatives, regardless of whether they were in the wedding party.

Pros: Remember those cousins and friends you couldn't fit into the wedding party? Putting them at your table makes them feel included—and makes you feel less guilty.

Cons: You'll have to displace some members of the wedding party, which might leave them feeling miffed. But if you place them with friends, they may not even notice.

4. The newlyweds sit with members of their immediate family.

Pros: It allows you to spend more time with your nearest and dearest.

Cons: All of the important players are concentrated at one table; seating the groom's parents at one table and the bride's parents at another makes it easier to spread out the "hosting" responsibilities. And if your family and hers are awkward around each other, this may not be the best time to force them to socialize.

If you'll be designating places for the rest of your guests (an approach which reduces the chaos when it's time for everyone to be seated), try to match up people with common interests or backgrounds who you think will enjoy one another's company. You should also be mindful of where the sound-system speakers will be situated, and avoid seating elderly guests near them.

Stepping Up

Unless you and your bride participate in the competitive ballroom dancing circuit, you probably don't know too many actual dance steps. Ordinarily, this doesn't matter. But in addition to having all those eyes on you, you're being photographed and/or taped, which means your grandchildren will see this someday. If there's ever a time to take a few lessons, this is it. Find a local dance instructor and tell him/her that you want to learn some basic moves for your first dance as husband and wife. Bring a CD that has your song on it. You don't need to learn thirty different dance styles. You need to learn one.

SELECTING THE SONG FOR YOUR FIRST DANCE

If you and your bride have a special song, you already know it. If nothing comes to mind, ask your band or DJ for a list of recommendations. Just keep the following pieces of advice in mind to make sure your first dance has all the right moves.

* Remember that you have to actually *dance* to the song. Ideally, you want something slow, since this is supposed to be a romantic dance, not a jitterbug. And some classic 1940s swing-era number might seem like a great idea, but it only works if you know how to swing. And don't ever choose "Stairway to Heaven." No one knows what to do when the fast part starts.

* Beware of anything too new. There's a good chance it will be overplayed and you'll be sick of it before long. If you're having the reception videotaped, you don't want to find yourself having to hit the mute button when you watch this part down the road. A timeless classic—or even something from three years ago—is always a better bet than a brand-new hit you might come to despise a week after your wedding.

* Listen to the lyrics. Plenty of beautiful, seemingly moving love songs are actually about relationships that have ended. Do you really want your first dance to be mournful? And then there's Eric Clapton's "Wonderful Tonight," the ultimate slow-dance favorite. But listen to the words: It's about a man who goes to a party, drinks too much, and has to be driven home and helped into bed by his significant other seconds before he passes out. In other words, it's a musical snapshot of a relationship about four seconds before it self-destructs.

TOASTS WITH THE MOST

Hopefully you've selected a best man who's somewhat responsible and not just a guy you sometimes drink with at 4:00 A.M. In all likelihood, you can trust him to offer a toast that's short and sentimental. But just in case you think he might be flaking on you, feel free to ask him how the speech is coming along and to check on the content. You have to do this carefully—it's his toast, after all. But there's nothing wrong with subtly offering a few guidelines. Mention that you went to a wedding a couple of years ago where the best man went on and on about the groom but never mentioned the bride, and how horrified everyone was. He'll make a mental note to praise your bride in his speech. And if you're at all concerned he'll mention past girlfriends or drunken escapades you'd rather not have revealed to two hundred people, go ahead and tell him to save those sorts of stories for your bachelor party.

If your best man isn't too sensitive, you may be able to get away with giving him some specific guidelines on his toast. If this is the case, here are a few tips to mention.

1. **Keep it short and sweet.** Nothing's worse than listening to the best man ramble on and on about your grade-school days while the guests face-dive into their salads.

2. **Don't leave anyone out.** Your best man should say something nice about you, something nice about your bride, and something nice about you as a couple.

3. **Use a cheat sheet.** Let him know that it's fine for him to refer to note cards if he has to. It's better than going blank and having to ad-lib.

4. **Remember that it's a toast.** At the end of the speech, glasses should be raised and some approximation of the words "So I'd like to propose a toast…" should be uttered.

5. **Go easy on the alcohol.** A good reason to schedule the toasts early in the reception is to guard against the best man getting blitzed before he speaks. Let him know that a drink or two is fine to calm nerves, but he should save the serious boozing for *after* his delivery of the toast.

6. **Humor is OK—but keep it PG.** You've got grandparents present, if not little kids. Make sure he realizes he's not just talking to his buddies. And sarcasm can easily be misunderstood, so when in doubt, he should choose heartfelt over humorous.

You, too, can choose to make a toast or brief speech during the reception, though speaking during the rehearsal dinner is more common. Your own speech doesn't need to be about you and your bride; it's an opportunity to thank guests for sharing your wedding with you and to thank your parents for all they've done.

Chapter Nine

Giving and Getting

At times, as you plan and plan and plan for an event that will be over in a matter of a several hours, it's tough to remember why you're going through it all. Two words: the loot—er, your bride. Of course. Your bride.

Still, a side benefit to this whole marriage thing is that you'll wind up with more gifts than you'll know what to do with. Along the way, you'll have to give some presents as well. This chapter covers all the booty (the pirate kind, not the J.Lo kind).

Where Most Men Fear to Tread: Registering

If you're like most guys, the thought of wandering among aisles of plate patterns fills you with dread. But think outside the china box: You can register for nontraditional items as well, such as TVs, DVD players, digital cameras—in other words, all the stuff you've been craving but didn't want to go into debt for. Here are some guidelines for loading up on the marital loot.

Cover the basics. You *are* about to start a home together, which means you need all the homey things—linens for the bedroom and bathroom, and at least eight place settings of formal tableware, glassware, and flatware. If you've already got decent everyday plates and glasses, there's no need to register for new ones. Wherever you go, a salesperson can help make sure you don't leave anything off your list.

Don't get too selfish. It's cool to suggest a stereo you'll both listen to. A Sony PlayStation that you'll use while she glares at you? That doesn't belong on the registry.

Express yourself. Sometimes—when it comes to choosing flowers for the reception centerpieces, for instance—you can probably get away with saying, "You know, honey, whatever you want will be fine." This is not one of those times. You're choosing items that you'll be living with for years, if not your whole lives.

Pick your battles. She wants floral-patterned china; you want a more modern look. What to do? Remember: It's all about compromise. Give way on the formal china, and select more modern everyday tableware. Or let her win out on all tableware and flatware decisions, so long as you get the final say on the martini glasses.

Be selective. Some stores offer discounts on registry items that you and your bride purchase yourselves after the wedding. Get the details: Some places only give you one chance to use the discount, others insist you complete a certain percentage of your registry in order to qualify, and all give you some time limit before the discount expires. This is precisely the sort of detail couples overlook when they're deciding where to register, but it's important. The more flexibility, the better.

Play it safe. Inquire about each store's policies regarding return, exchange, and replacement (for items that arrive damaged); make sure that you're comfortable with the procedure and that it's not too inconvenient.

Be practical. A common mistake: registering for enough barware to fill every joint on Bourbon Street. Before you add on the brandy snifters, ask yourself, "Do I even *like* brandy?"

Show your range. If you register only at high-end stores, guests who want to spend less will skip your registry and wind up getting you a vase. An ugly vase. Register at a few different places, for items both extravagant and economical, so that all of your guests will have options they're comfortable with.

Take the road less traveled. Of course, you don't have to register at all. If you'd prefer to get good ol' cash, you can discreetly put the word out that you're accepting contributions for a new home or a honeymoon fund (however, just saying "We want cash" is taboo). As mentioned in the honeymoon chapter, some travel agencies offer registries that allow guests to give money toward a honeymoon. But be prepared: Many guests consider cash too impersonal and will insist on buying you something—and if you haven't registered, it will be something *they* like. Other couples choose a charity and request that guests make donations instead of giving gifts—a generous gesture, so long as you don't pick a divisive or political cause that might make guests uncomfortable.

GIFTS FOR GROOMSMEN

Your groomsmen may not be doing much for you. While your best man gets stuck throwing a bachelor party and giving speeches, the rest of them may just be wearing a nice outfit and hoping to hook up with a bridesmaid. Still, you have to do something for your best man and the rest of the crew.

Giving gifts to your attendants is a way to express gratitude for their help during your wedding. More importantly, it's a way to

 Guru Grooms on...

Registering

"We felt like we *had* to register for all the traditional things, even if we didn't need them. For example, we already had twelve champagne glasses between us, but we registered for six more. How often do you have a champagne toast for eighteen–are you hosting your own wedding? If I could do it differently, I would have registered for more practical items–like towels and a new lawnmower."

—Andy, 35, Arlington, VA

express gratitude for years of friendship, to let them know that you don't take them for granted, despite appearances to the contrary. Don't worry: Rolexes are not expected. In general, these gifts tend to adhere to certain guidelines.

* They're small and relatively inexpensive, since you're giving out a bunch of them.

* They're supposed to look semiclassy and last a long time, so they tend to be silver, metal, or leather rather than plastic.

* They're often engraved with the name or initials of the recipient, which adds a personal touch.

* They don't need to be identical, though you should spend the same amount on each groomsman—and a little more on your best man, since he's doing all of the work.

* They should be handed out at your rehearsal dinner—not your bachelor party—when the guys are likely to remain conscious.

WHAT TO GET

* Flasks. They're not very practical—honestly, how often does anyone drink out of a flask?—but guys like 'em nonetheless.

* Lighters. The disposable plastic variety is a bad idea, but a fancy silver lighter makes a nice gift. Just stay away from lighters specifically meant for cigars; if your groomsmen don't smoke, that's a totally useless gift. Otherwise, lighters can be used by anyone.

* Martini shakers. As with flasks, whether or not your friends are likely to sit at home whipping up martinis is irrelevant. Shakers look good on a bar, are practical for parties, and help men pretend they're Hugh Hefner—the eternal male fantasy.

* Minibar sets, which come in handy at parties, or wine opener and bottle stopper sets, which are perfect for personal use too.

* Money clips. Paying for things with a roll of bills tucked into a silver money clip allows your friends to have a brief illusion of wealth and power. For that, they'll be grateful.

* MP3 players. Small, low-memory versions are surprisingly cheap and make perfect companions at the gym.

* Luggage tags. If you're making people travel to your wedding, silver-plated, engraved luggage tags are not only useful but seem like a particularly thoughtful way to thank your groomsmen for coming. Other options: monogrammed travel bags or toiletry kits.

* Swiss Army knives. They're often too small to engrave, but they're always practical.

* Distinctive beer steins or martini glasses, glass or pewter beer mugs, or sets of shot glasses.

* Engraved wooden wine boxes or sets of classy coasters.

* Fine bottles of wine or champagne—or, if you're splurging, memberships in a beer- or wine-of-the-month club.

* Sets of cuff links or tuxedo studs. Your groomsmen will look good on your wedding day and end up with a practical parting gift.

* Silver or leather key rings, leather wallets, or engraved business card holders.

* Desk accessories, such as clocks or silver pen-and-pencil sets.

* Barbecue utensil sets.

* Classic, old-fashioned shaving kits.

* Gift certificates. They seem impersonal, but if you get each groomsman a gift certificate to a restaurant near his home, it shows you put in a little effort.

What Not to Get

* Humidors, cigar-cutting sets, and cigar holders are great, but only if your friends smoke cigars. Ditto a box of fancy cigars.

* Something related to a single sport. You may be a golf fanatic, but are all of your groomsmen? Think before you buy them silver golf tees or monogrammed baseball bats. Mixing and matching—a golf club for one friend, a new catcher's mitt for another—can solve this problem.

* Tickets to a big game or concert. This sounds great, and it's a chance for you all to bond in the future. But you've already made your friends schedule time for your bachelor party, rehearsal dinner, and wedding—expecting everyone to get together again in a few months is a bit much.

Thank-You Gifts for Your Parents

If both sets of parents have shouldered the cost of the wedding, you've got a lot to thank them for. But even if they haven't, they are responsible for, at a minimum, your creation and/or upbringing. As they prepare to send you off into married life, this is your opportunity to give them a token of appreciation. The only ground rule is that you give them something they can use together—in other words, not a hunting rifle for your dad and perfume for your mom.

Your rehearsal dinner is probably the best time to give them their gift, since you'll all have too much going on at your wedding. Some possible presents include:

* A gift certificate to their favorite restaurant.

* A gift certificate for a night or weekend at an inn or bed-and-breakfast.

* A couples spa treatment.

* Tickets to a show or concert.

* Membership at a museum they enjoy.

* An extravagant bouquet of flowers for their home.

* A framed photo of your parents with you and your bride.

* A wedding album designed just for them (ditch the photos of your friends and replace them with family instead).

* An engraved silver picture frame.

* A framed wedding invitation.

GIFT FOR YOUR BRIDE

By now, you're fed up. Getting married is supposed to be about *getting* gifts, not giving them. Here's some good news: Many couples have abandoned the practice of buying each other gifts. Instead, they make their honeymoon or wedding rings a mutual gift. Or they simply decide they're better off saving the money so they can pay the electricity bills.

If you decide to give each other wedding gifts, however, keep in mind that your bride is not one of your groomsmen. A flask won't cut it. Ideally, you should get her something personal. Think about her hobbies. If she's addicted to romance novels, how about a romance-of-the-month club membership? If she gardens, get her gardening tools and bulbs to plant. If she's an athlete, get her something she can use for her favorite sport. If you're still having a hard time, here are some ideas that should keep you out of trouble.

* Jewelry. Keep it simple and understated, since you've recently spent a small fortune on the engagement ring. Try elegant earrings or a pearl necklace.

* A gift certificate for a massage, facial, or pedicure. Or splurge on a day at a spa. It will help her de-stress a few weeks from now when she discovers what a slob you really are.

* A bouquet of flowers in a fancy vase.

* A music box or jewelry box.

* Dinner at a posh restaurant.

* Tickets to a show or to see her favorite performer.

* A weekend at a romantic hotel to be used on your six-month anniversary.

* A basket of boutique bath and body products, from soaps to body lotion to perfume.

* A pair of silk slippers.

* A ridiculously expensive bottle of champagne and two crystal champagne flutes.

* Looking to save money? Write her a sappy poem or cook her dinner.

PAYBACK: WRITING THANK-YOU NOTES

Remember how much fun you had picking out all those gifts for your registry? Now you have to thank everyone who got you something. If they got you a full set of china, you have to thank them. If they got you a single beer mug despite making three times your income, you have to thank them. And you have to thank them in writing. On classy stationery:

Yes, this task feels like a chore, and nobody likes doing it—not even your bride, so you can't make her shoulder the burden. You should roughly split the duties. The worst thing you can do is procrastinate so that you've got to write one hundred thank-you notes in a single weekend. As you receive gifts, keep a list of who sent what when, and try to send out notes within a month. Below are a few noteworthy points for writing thank-you notes.

1. Be specific. The fear of every guest who gets you something from a registry is that you can't actually remember who got you what (which, of course, you can't). Your thank-you note should mention what the gift was: a glass vase, a set of fine china, a beer mug.

2. Don't be *too* specific. Sometimes a store will send you a note informing you that Mr. and Mrs. So-and-So have purchased you a set of silverware that is currently on back order. So you're writing notes for items you haven't even seen yet. You don't want the gift-givers to know this. So don't describe their gift as "a set of twelve stainless-steel silverware pieces with a floral decoration on the handles." You'll sound like a catalog.

3. Embrace adjectives. Alas, you can't simply thank people for a vase. You have to thank them for a gorgeous vase. An elegant vase. A colorful vase. This holds true no matter what the gift. A DVD player? It's cutting-edge, top-of-the-line, or plain ol' fantastic. Invest in a thesaurus.

4. Go above and beyond "thank you." If they got you that vase, let them know you've already found the ideal spot for it on the mantel in your living room. If it's an item of furniture, mention how perfectly it fits in with your home. If it's a DVD player, you've already run out to buy *The Matrix*. The idea is to make the guest think, "Gosh, I got them the best gift ever," regardless of what you really think of the item.

5. Avoid the "M" word. That's "money," not "marriage." Never mention money (or cash or checks, for that matter) by name. If they got you moola, you should thank them for their "generous gift" or "thoughtful gift."

6. Know your reader. Writing two hundred eerily similar notes is enough to drive anyone over the edge. When you're thanking your best friend from college, take the opportunity to throw out the formula and relax. If he got you barware, tell him you expect him to come over after you're back from the honeymoon and use each and every glass until you're both sick. (If your best friend from college is a recovering alcoholic, do not do this.) Consider it a break from the other notes.

7. Mention the wedding. If you're writing your notes to gift-givers before the big day, say how much you're looking forward to seeing them. If it's after, thank them for sharing your wedding day with you, and mention that having them there made the day even more special. And if they couldn't make it, tell them how sorry you were not to see them.

8. Make it from both of you. Even if you're writing to your best pal, "I" should not appear in a thank-you note. It's all about "we." And no matter who writes the cards, you should both sign your names for that personal touch.

SAMPLE NOTES

Right:

Dear Aunt Ethel and Uncle Phil,

Thank you so much for the beautiful set of dishes. We can finally throw out the cracked ones we've had since college. As soon as we've settled in to the new place, we'll have you over for dinner so we can put them to good use!

It was wonderful seeing you at the wedding. Having you both there made the day truly special for us. We can't wait to see you at Thanksgiving!

Love,

You and Your Better Half

Wrong:

Dear Aunt Ethel and Uncle Phil,

Thanks so much for the set of ceramic dishes with floral weave pattern #7514-3A. They are nice. See you soon,

You and Your Better Half

(who will no longer be invited

to Thanksgiving)

Chapter Ten

The *Really* Fun Stuff
The Bachelor Party

Consider this your reward for being the perfect groom. (You have been the perfect groom, right?) Your bachelor party is a chance to take a legally sanctioned time-out from wedding planning and spend an afternoon or evening—or both—hanging out with your guy friends, doing guy stuff, and *not* thinking about your bride.

Which means it's also a chance to screw everything up and to do something astoundingly stupid that comes back to haunt you.

That's the tricky part. Chances are your bride won't approve of whatever you're doing at your bachelor party, unless it's totally G-rated. A little disapproval is all right—most women will eventually forgive you if you come home inebriated and reeking of cigar smoke. Most women will *not* forgive you if you come home reeking of perfume. Hopefully your own moral compass will guide you.

Typically, your best man—with or without some help from your other groomsmen—plans the bachelor party. Sometimes the event is a surprise. In other instances, the best man consults the groom, so be prepared with a list of whom you'd like to invite, as well as some dates that work for you. If there are certain situations that you want to avoid—such as having the party the night before the wedding or having naked girls be part of the festivities—casually get this point across without making it seem like you're expecting your best man to put together some sort of event for you.

Whom to Invite

* As opposed to your wedding, when you're trying to please your family and your bride, the bachelor party is all about you. You can include whomever you want—from your five closest friends to thirty pals and relatives.

* That said, don't go overboard; guests at your bachelor party should be people you genuinely want to see, not casual acquaintances or coworkers you feel required to invite.

* Some guys choose to include the bride's siblings—or even her father. If you're planning to take in a baseball game, this is fine. If you're going to a strip club, no one related to your future wife should be there. You'll end up spending the whole night feeling uncomfortable and looking over your shoulder, when the whole point of your bachelor party is to have fun.

WHEN TO HAVE IT

Rule number one: Do not have the bachelor party the night before the wedding. Rule number two: Reread rule number one. Repeat. Memorize. Carve into your flesh.

This seems like a no-brainer, but men persist in ignoring this bit of common sense. Thus, all over the country, as grooms are standing at the altar in front of friends and family, gazing into the eyes of their beloved, they're having the same thought: "Oh Lord, please don't let me hurl." Or worse: "Oh Lord, I think I'm gonna hurl." Or the worst: "Oh Lord, I can't believe I just hurled."

These are not the thoughts you want to be having on your wedding day.

Aside from that, a bachelor party can take place anytime: two months, two weeks, or two days before the wedding. Your best man

 Guru Grooms on...

Bad Bachelor Party Timing

"My bride had agreed to any type of party I wanted on one condition—that it not be held the night before the wedding. Naturally, after the rehearsal dinner—the night before the wedding—a group of friends took me out to a strip club, where there was much drinking. The next day, the mere smell of alcohol almost did me in. Managing to make it through the day without throwing up was a major accomplishment."

—Len, 37, Philadelphia

should ask you what dates work for you, then float them by the other groomsmen to figure out what's most convenient.

What to Do

A bachelor party can take many different forms. The most common tend to involve some combination of the three Bs: beef, booze, and broads. (It's not very PC, but neither is a bachelor party.) That said, you can still have a great time without any of these staples. Here are some ideas you can suggest to the organizer if you're asked for input.

The Classic. Start with dinner at a steak joint (or any establishment that reeks of testosterone), and keep the red wine flowing. After dinner, make your way to a strip club for an hour or two. Finally, adjourn to a friend's bachelor pad—or a hotel suite that doubles as a crash pad for out-of-towners—for a little poker, scotch, and stogies. It's manly and classy. You could almost be in the Rat Pack.

The Weekend Warrior. Every guy dreams of spending a bachelor weekend in Vegas or New Orleans. It isn't easy to pull off, though, since your close friends are already giving up a weekend for your wedding, and the additional time and money required for another getaway may force some friends to drop out. Atlantic City doesn't have the same cachet as Vegas, but it's cheaper and, if you're on the East Coast, a lot more convenient. A golf/beach/ski resort is another great weekend destination.

The Barfly. Rent out a bar—a swank spot, a total dive, or a karaoke room—for the night. Added bonus: the feeling of power as non-invitees are turned away.

The Team Player. Spend an afternoon on the golf course. Get a group together for a game of basketball, football, or baseball. Or try skiing, sailing, or whitewater rafting. That way, when you eat a pound of meat at dinner, you can feel like you earned it.

The Fan Favorite. Attend a sporting event or head to the racetrack, and spend the afternoon watching other people exert themselves while you drink beer and eat peanuts. Or check out a rock concert or a local jazz band instead.

The Neanderthal. Regress to your prehistoric roots and go hunting or fishing for an afternoon—or add camping and turn it into a weekend excursion. Occasionally beat your chest with your fists and grunt to complete the image.

The Ol' College Try. Relive your university days with a bar crawl. *Crawl* is the important word here; unless you've got a designated driver or you hire a car to take you around, do this on foot.

The Game Boy. Play laser tag or paintball, or hit a video arcade. If you like your reality less virtual, head to a bowling alley or pool hall, or go go-cart racing.

The Lazy Man. Get together at someone's house. Order pizza. Drink beer. Watch a season of *The Sopranos* on DVD. As long as you're hanging out with your best friends, who cares what you do?

 Guru Grooms on...

Just Saying No

"The bachelor parties I've been to have mostly been fun, but sometimes it seems like there's some anxiety–like people are worried they're not partying hard enough for a bachelor party. I really didn't want one, so I didn't have one."

—Steve, 30, Los Angeles

STRIP CLUB CLASS

For some reason, Emily Post never covered proper etiquette for a strip club. Luckily, you've got this book. If you've never been to a, uh, gentleman's establishment, you may be thinking, "Oh, come on—anything goes." Not exactly. You see, besides the naked women, there are some other extremely important people who work at strip clubs: large, glowering men. Their job: to forcibly remove you from the premises if you do anything you shouldn't. To avoid a run-in with said men, here are some basic ground rules for how to act at a strip club.

1. Look, but don't touch. Even if you don't want a lap dance, your evil friends may buy one for you. Pretend you're on an amusement park ride. Do whatever you need to, but remember: Keep your arms at your sides at all times. So long as you remain passive, you can look your fiancée in the eye later on and say, "Honey, I didn't do anything wrong." The instant you make any sort of physical contact, two people have legitimate reasons to wish you bodily harm: your bride-to-be and the enormous bouncer rushing toward you with a crowbar.

2. Be polite. Whether you're getting a lap dance or just being served a drink, being in a strip club doesn't give you license to act like a caveman. Say "please" and "thank you." And if your fiancée forbade you from getting lap dances, don't recoil in horror when a woman approaches and asks if you'd like one. A smile and a "no thank you" should suffice. If she's persistent or acts wounded, tell the truth: "I'd love to, but my fiancée told me I couldn't." You'll instantly be declared the nicest guy in the place.

3. Tip, and tip well. You don't need to tip after a lap dance—it costs enough to begin with. You do need to tip your waitress when she brings you drinks. And look around—if you're in one of those joints where the patrons give dollar bills to the women on stage, do the same.

4. Don't fall in love. It's an absurdly common phenomenon: Stripper dances for man. Stripper chats a bit with man. Stripper laughs at man's jokes, gazes deep into man's eyes, tells man he's different from the other guys in the club. Man believes all of it. Man thinks, "Wow, she *really* likes me." Man imagines life with stripper. Man has been had. Remember: It's her job to make you think she likes you so you'll spend more money on her. She doesn't really like you. Your fiancée, on the other hand, does. Be aware of the difference.

How to Have Fun—Without Destroying Your Marriage

* Understand that this is *not* your last hurrah. There's a sort of pressure to go wild at your bachelor party because after this you'll supposedly never have a chance to go out with your friends again. This is nonsense. Believe it or not, you will see your male friends after you're married. You can even have guys' nights out. And you'll no doubt go to other friends' bachelor parties. So there's no need to fit a lifetime of decadence into one night.

* Picture your bride doing what you're doing. Imagine your fiancée and a bunch of her friends watching some guy strip on stage. No biggie? Cool—go to a strip club and have fun. But wait: Now imagine that naked guy straddling your bride and writhing. A little upsetting? Then maybe you should skip the lap dance. If you're uncomfortable with your fiancée doing something, you shouldn't be doing it either.

The Bridal Shower—What's Your Role?

While most brides don't want the groom to have anything to do with the shower, some do want him to put in an appearance. This simply entails popping in for the final half hour or so of the shower (after the women have spent the day opening gifts), making the rounds, telling the guests how much you're looking forward to seeing them at the wedding, and helping your bride get all of the gifts home. It's over before you know it. If your bride is particularly cruel, she may insist on having a coed shower. In that case, you'll most likely have to smile relentlessly, open many gifts—oohing and aahing over each one—and be charming for a few hours. If you're lucky, the event will have been designed to appeal to both sexes and will involve an afternoon of bowling, a wine tasting, or something equally painless (and if you're really lucky, the gift-opening marathon will be skipped altogether—a guy can dream).

* Water down the booze. Unless you're a teetotaler, you'll be drinking at your bachelor party. You may be drinking more than you're used to. The last thing you want is to black out, then turn on the TV a few weeks later to see yourself stumbling around naked on an episode of *Cops*. A couple ways to minimize the damage: Make sure you eat something *before* you start drinking, and down one full glass of water for every alcoholic beverage you consume.

* If you don't trust yourself, don't tempt yourself. A strip club is full of bouncers to keep you in line. If your best man hires some escorts to party with you in a hotel room, *you're* the only one keeping you in line. If you think you can't be trusted to do the right thing, don't put yourself in that situation to begin with.

* Talk to your bride. Find out what she's comfortable with and what offends her. She may be fine with the idea that, just this once, your friends are going to drag you to a strip club. But the idea of having strippers in a hotel room might be too much for her. If it's going to cause real strain in your relationship, it isn't worth it.

* Talk to the host. Be very, very clear with your best man and anyone else planning your party. They may feel they have to throw the wildest party ever, while you'd be perfectly happy just hanging out and playing poker. If certain things are off-limits, say so in advance.

So, What's Your Bride Doing at Her Bachelorette Party?

Chances are, when you think of your bride out with her female friends, you picture them renting *Steel Magnolias* and weeping together. Or making a group quilt. Or, if they're really wild, whipping up cosmopolitans and reminiscing about their favorite episodes of *Sex and the City*.

And while it's entirely possible that they are, in fact, doing these things—except for the quilting—they may be doing much more. These days, bachelorette parties often replicate bachelor parties, which means one thing: There are plenty of places out there where women can go see guys do the full monty.

So what can your lovely fiancée do at a strip club? Everything you can. Another common bachelorette party practice: bar-hopping and seeing how many kisses (on the cheek, hopefully) the bride can get from guys she meets. If this upsets you—and if it doesn't, you're a remarkably open-minded kinda guy—set ground rules. Talk to your bride about your bachelor and bachelorette parties, and decide what's acceptable and what's not. But remember: What isn't good for the goose isn't good for the gander.

Chapter Eleven

The Big Day

It is finally here. The moment of joy. The moment of reckoning. It's time for the planning to stop and the doing to start.

THE WEDDING DAY AT A GLANCE

Honestly, by this point, your biggest responsibility is showing up and saying your vows. Here's a quick overview of what you'll have to do on this momentous day.

* Get dressed—correctly. Have your best man (or your parents) look you over before you head to the ceremony site. Remember your cuff links, studs, and any other extras that could fall through the cracks. If you're supposed to wear a boutonniere, be sure to do so. And if you're having a late-day wedding and you're prone to five o'clock shadow, give yourself a quick touch-up with an electric razor—or, if you're very careful, a regular blade.

* Give thanks where thanks are due. Take a minute to pull your parents aside and express your gratitude for all that they've done. It's the sort of thing you're liable to forget once the wedding madness begins.

* Remember the money. Give an envelope with the payment for the officiant and any other vendors you're responsible for paying to the best man or whomever you've designated to be the cash carrier.

* Remember the marriage license. Bring it yourself, or if you trust him enough, delegate this responsibility to the best man. This

document will need to be signed by the officiant and at least one witness after the ceremony. Without it, you're not married.

* If you've been holding on to your fiancée's wedding ring, hand it off to your best man—before the ceremony begins.

* Participate in the photo shoot for formal portraits (depending on how superstitious you and your bride are, this can take place before or after the ceremony—or some shots can be taken before and some after).

* Avoid collapsing during the ceremony.

* Recite your vows. Look at your bride when you say them, not the crowd.

* Kiss the bride. Sure, you're nervous, but make it more than a quick peck. On the other hand, anything that causes guests to shout "Get a room" is going too far.

* Greet guests in a receiving line, if you're having one.

* Dance with your bride at the reception. More than once. Even if you hate to dance.

* Dance with your mother while your bride dances with her dad. You can then mix it up, so that you're dancing with your mother-in-law while your bride dances with your father.

* Eat. Don't forget to do this.

* Schmooze with guests.

* Cut the cake. Feed a piece to your new wife. Do not shove the cake into her face, no matter how hilarious you think that would be.

* Give a toast thanking your parents and guests—if you've chosen to do so. Keep it brief and sentimental.

* Avoid collapsing during the reception.

* Ride off into the sunset (or the wee hours of the morning) with your bride.

So, What Do I Do All Day?

Your bride has a lot to keep her busy on the wedding day: makeup, hair, mysterious female bonding rituals with her bridesmaids. You, on the other hand, may have time on your hands. Sitting and staring at a wall for four hours before your wedding is a remarkably bad idea. But whatever you end up doing, don't stray too far from the wedding site or lose track of time. Figure out precisely when you need to start getting ready, then set an alarm in case your own internal clock fails, and ask your best man to make sure to remind you when the time comes as well. Here are some ways to spend the hours before you walk down the aisle.

Exert yourself. Head to the gym or go for a jog to work off some of your nervous energy.

Be a team player. Get together with a group of friends for some baseball, football, basketball, or golf.

Rent a movie. Round up a few pals and watch something funny like *Austin Powers* or *Airplane*.

Eat. Despite being surrounded by food at your wedding, you may have little opportunity to actually sit down and ingest it. So have a decent-size lunch or even a small prewedding dinner to help you make it through the event.

Take a nap. If you're able to relax enough, twenty minutes of sleep can leave you refreshed and energized for the big night. But set an alarm. Better yet, set *two* alarms.

Get Ready, Get Set

You don't want to be dressed and ready to go three hours before you're supposed to show up for photos. Nor do you want to be frantically fumbling with your cuff links six minutes before the ceremony begins. It's better to err on the side of too much time. If it normally takes you an hour to shower and get ready for work in the morning, give yourself at least an extra half hour just this once. If you're going to tie your own bow tie, allow yourself an additional six hours to accomplish this task successfully.

STRESS MANAGEMENT TIPS

Your heart is racing. Your head is throbbing. As the moment of your matrimony approaches, you may be feeling a massive amount of stress. Here are some steps to help you relax.

* Acknowledge the stress—and realize how normal it is. The worst way to cope with fear and panic is to pretend it's not there. Accept it: You're freaking out a bit, as has every groom in all of recorded history. There's nothing wrong with you.

* Don't hide it from your bride. You're going through this together, so don't be afraid to talk about it.

* Exercise, exercise, exercise. The simplest and most immediate way to de-stress—aside from getting staggeringly drunk, an incredibly bad idea at this point—is to shift that stress from your mind to your body. Find some time, even during these busy few days, to get active. Go for a jog, or take a long walk. Lift weights. Play tennis. Swim laps. Beat the crap out of a punching bag. Anything that will use up some of that nervous energy and take your mind off the wedding will help. (If your most strenuous activity of late has been pressing the buttons on your remote control, take it easy—you don't want to pull a muscle on the day of your wedding.)

* Slow down. If you're into meditation, this is the time to practice it. If you're not, just force yourself to take some time out of your day to be alone. Find a quiet place, put on your favorite CD, take deep breaths, and attempt to empty your mind. It's not easy, but try focusing on the music or listening to yourself breathe. Or pick a word, and recite it over and over like a mantra. (That word should not be "wedding" or "marriage.")

* Picture the positive. Close your eyes and imagine yourself doing whatever makes you happy—lying on a beach, say, or winning the lottery.

* If you're having cold feet, picture all of the happy times you've had with your bride—unrelated to your wedding. Imagine your first date or a vacation you took together. Or just picture a typical afternoon for the two of you. Remember: that won't change after you're married.

* Breathe. Sure, you tend to do this anyway, but deep breathing techniques are proven de-stressors. Take long, slow, deep breaths—in through your nose, out through your mouth—and imagine your stress leaving your body every time you exhale.

* Cut down on caffeine. If you're feeling jittery, that fourth cup of coffee will only make it worse. You've got more adrenaline coursing through your system than you usually do anyway, so you're unlikely to need artificial stimulation. On the other hand, this isn't the time to quit cold turkey. If you have a cup of coffee every morning, don't stop now, but consider limiting your intake.

* Check out the spa. If you're staying at a hotel for your wedding, see if massages are offered. Or spend a little time in the steam room or sauna.

* Keep reminding yourself that, before long, you'll be on your honeymoon.

* Practice. Ideally, you want to take your mind off your wedding for a few hours. But if that's impossible, it may reassure you to get your best man and groomsmen together and go over all your roles in the ceremony and reception one more time.

* Don't expect perfection. If you've been to a few weddings and rehearsal dinners, you've seen mishaps. A waiter dropped a tray of food. The DJ mispronounced the names of the bride and groom when introducing them. Somebody blanked in the middle of a toast and stood there turning red. And, aside from the bride and groom, no one really cared. Your guests will have a good time no matter what happens. Your friends and family are there to eat, drink, hang out with their pals, and wish you well.

 Guru Grooms on...

Close Calls

"The morning of the wedding, I went sailing with friends on a small Pennsylvania lake. Someone dropped us off, and when we paddled to shore, I realized there was nobody around to drive me back. I had to run two miles to the place my future wife was staying and get one of her friends to give me a ride to where I was staying. I barely made it to the ceremony on time."

—*Steve, 41, Brooklyn, NY*

MEET AND GREET: THE RECEIVING LINE

So you've exchanged vows, and you and your bride have been pronounced husband and wife. All of the guests want to congratulate you. The receiving line offers an opportunity for them to do this. This ritual—which is by no means obligatory—can take place either at the ceremony site as the guests file out or at the reception venue as they enter the party space. The alternative is to circulate from table to table during the reception, making sure to thank each and every person for coming. Regardless of which approach you prefer, you and your bride must put in a little personal face time with all of your guests individually. These people made an effort to come to your wedding; it's the least you can do. Your bride, undoubtedly, will know all of the etiquette rules regarding who stands where in a receiving line. Here's what you should be aware of.

What to do: Smile. Shake the hands of the men, and kiss the cheeks of the women. Look them in the eye, exchange brief pleasantries, and thank them for coming. If you think you're *supposed* to know someone's name and you're blanking, make your greeting especially enthusiastic to cover it.

What not to do: Don't chat about the weather, sports, or anything else, or the other people waiting in line may begin to riot. Don't be rude and cut people off mid-sentence, but attempt to move them along. "We'll see you at the reception" or "We'll talk to you more at the reception" is a polite way to keep things rolling.

What are the advantages? The receiving line provides an organized way for you and your families to greet each and every person, giving you a better chance of not missing anyone who might feel slighted.

What are the disadvantages? This ritual can be tedious—for both you and your guests. Friends and family are forced to wait patiently in line for their five seconds with you when all they really want to do is head to the bar and dig into the hors d'oeuvres.

What's a couple to do? If you have a large guest list, you may want to forgo the receiving line, since the greater the number of people, the longer the whole process will take. The alternative, as mentioned earlier, is for you and your bride (and, separately, the hosts of the wedding) to make the rounds from table to table, personally greeting and thanking each individual. This approach is generally less painful and more relaxing for your guests (and, possibly, for you too); however, it means you're spending more of the reception taking care of "obligations," as opposed to missing most of the cocktail hour. Keep in mind that the hosts of the wedding will most likely have their own ideas about how this aspect of the event should be handled.

THE FIRST DANCE

While the pressure is off for the most part once the party starts, you still need to make it through your first dance. This is yet another moment when you and your bride stand alone in the spotlight while hundreds of people stare at you. Here are some tips to make things go smoothly.

Loosen up. Many couples are so concerned with remembering their dance steps that they move stiffly and stare straight ahead with looks of pained concentration on their faces. Remember that you're supposed to be enjoying yourselves. Look into your wife's eyes while you dance. Smile at her. Whisper in her ear, even just to say, "Um, honey, I've completely forgotten everything that useless dance instructor taught us."

Stay close. Don't hold each other at arm's length while you're dancing. You're married now.

Laugh. You just stepped on her feet. She just kneed you in the groin (accidentally, you hope). You've forgotten the routine you carefully memorized. You're starting to panic. When all else fails, laugh at yourself. Ham it up a little if you want, or dip your bride and give her a passionate kiss. Or just start guffawing. As long as you look like you're having fun, your guests will cheer and think, "What a lovely, uncoordinated couple."

How to Behave at the Reception

It's time to breathe easy, knock back a few drinks, cut loose on the dance floor, and just enjoy yourself. Really. You're supposed to have fun at your reception, so relax. Still, there are a few ground rules for how to act during this party to end all parties.

1. Don't drink too much. This can't possibly be overstated. You rarely get the chance to eat a lot at your wedding, but the booze is flowing, which means you're liable to get inebriated a lot faster than usual. By all means, enjoy yourself, but be careful.

2. Don't forget to schmooze. It's tempting to spend all night dancing with your wife or hanging out with high school buddies you haven't seen in ages. But it's important to spread the love and socialize with the rest of your guests, some of whom probably made a big effort to attend.

3. Don't neglect your bride. Some couples split up to better work the room. Some couples split up because they're each busy catching up with old friends. Both situations are fine. But stop every so often throughout the reception and connect with your bride. Take a turn together on the dance floor, or simply retreat to your table and grab a bite to eat. She is, after all, the reason you went through all of this.

After the Big Day

Congratulations!
You made it. You're husband and wife.

WHO NEEDS TO KNOW?

If your wife is taking your last name, she'll need to apply for a new social security card and driver's license, then follow up with new credit cards, passport, voter registration card, and so on. You've got it a lot easier. But there are still people you need to notify on your end.

* **HR.** Contact the human resources office at your workplace. Tell them you've gotten married, and ask what forms you need to fill out. Whatever information they have on you for tax purposes should be updated to show that you're married. You may also want to look into having your wife covered on your company's medical and dental insurance or getting yourself onto hers.

* **Insurance companies.** Notify these agencies of your change in marital status, and make the appropriate changes to policies so that your wife is covered on yours or you on hers. You'll probably want to make her the primary beneficiary, where applicable, as well.

* **Savings accounts.** Similarly, you'll most likely want to update your retirement and investment accounts (IRAs, 401(k)s, money market accounts) so that your wife is the primary beneficiary.

* **Money managers.** Notify any accountants/financial planners/ tax preparers either of you use. All income tax forms you file after you're married should reflect your wedded status.

HAPPILY EVER AFTER

Once the madness of wedding planning is behind you—and you've finally finished writing thank-you notes—you'll be thrilled to settle back into the routine of life. But you don't want the marriage itself to become routine. Keeping your relationship feeling fresh and passionate is the subject of another book—actually, hundreds of them.

But here are a few ways to keep your romance going strong in the years ahead.

Continue to date. No, not other people—each other. Just because you're married doesn't mean you should spend every night sitting at home watching television. Go out for a nice dinner. See a show. Go dancing. Don't wait for an occasion.

Surprise her. It's inevitable: Married life settles into a pattern. So pick her up on a random Friday and whisk her off for a weekend in Paris—or to a nearby bed-and-breakfast.

Make time for each other. Life can be so hectic that you feel as if you barely see your own spouse. Meet for lunch once a week, or set your alarm a half hour earlier than you need to in the mornings.

Give each other some space. You're a couple, but you're still individuals. Go out with your guy friends every now and then, and encourage her to go out with the gals.

Use your wedding planning skills. Remember how good you got at compromising and communicating? You'll need to use those abilities for the rest of your life.

Don't ever forget your anniversary. 'Nuff said.

Marriage, like everything else, has highs and lows, and in the years ahead, you and your wife will know plenty of both. That said, once you've made it through the ordeal known as wedding planning, marriage itself is a piece of cake.

Notes

Notes

Index

Ascots, 76
Attire, 70–83
    for groom, 71–82
    for groomsmen, 82–83
    renting versus buying, 78–79

Bachelor party, 145–153
Bachelorette party, 153
Band, for reception, 62–66
Best man, 50–53, 114, 130–131
Boutonnieres, 76
Bridal shower, 152–153
Bride
    gifts for, 140–141
    responsibilities of, 7, 66–67
Budget, 32–42

Carat, of diamonds, 20
Caterer, 111
Ceremony, 56–62
    civil, 57–58, 59
    religious, 56–59
    site of, 44–46
    writing vows for, 60–62
Children, at wedding, 50
Civil ceremony, 57–58, 59
Clarity, of diamonds, 17–18
Clothing. See attire
Color, of diamonds, 18–19
Communication, 32
Contracts
    with band/DJ, 65–66
    for rented attire, 82
    for transportation, 123–124
Cruise, for honeymoon, 101–102
Cuff links, 76
Culture, 59–60
Cummerbunds, 76
Cut, of diamonds, 19–20

Date, setting of, 42–44
Destination weddings, 44–45

Diamonds, 16–23
DJ, for reception, 62–66

Engagement, 15–30
Engagement party, 29–30
Engagement rings, 16–23
Entertainment, for rehearsal dinner, 113
Ethnicity, 59–60

Finances. See budget
First dance, 129–130, 164–165

Gift registry, 94, 134–137
Gifts
    for bride, 140–141
    for groomsmen, 136–139
    for out-of-town guests, 116
    for parents, 139–140
    at rehearsal dinner, 113
Groom
    attire for, 71–82
    responsibilities of, 7–8
    toast from, 131
Groomsmen
    attire for, 82–83
    gifts for, 136–139
    selection of, 53–54
Guest list
    for rehearsal dinner, 106
    for wedding, 45, 48–50
Guests, activities for, 115–116

Holiday weddings, 43–44
Honeymoon, 44, 85–102
    destination of, 89–93
    dos and don'ts, 95–97
    hotel accommodations, 100–101
    money-saving tips, 93–95
    planning timeline, 86–88
    travel agent for, 98–99
Hotel accommodations
    for honeymoon, 100–101
    for out-of-town guests, 116

In-laws
    first meeting with, 27–28
    talking to before proposal, 24
Insurance
    for engagement ring, 16
    for wedding, 42
Interfaith ceremony, 58–59
Invitations
    for rehearsal dinner, 112
    for wedding, 67

Liability insurance, 42

Maid of honor, 114
Marriage license, 124–125
Music
    for first dance, 129–130
    at reception, 62–66

Officiants
    for civil ceremony, 57–58
    for religious ceremony, 56–57
    and site selection, 45
Outdoor weddings, 44, 46

Parents
    gifts for, 139–140
    meeting of, 27
    and wedding budget, 33–35
Pocket squares, 77
Post-wedding activities, 168–169
Proposal, 17, 23–26

Receiving line, 162–164
Reception
    behavior at, 165
    culture/ethnicity and, 60
    first dance at, 129–130, 164–165
    formal versus informal, 45
    music at, 62–66
    seating arrangements for,
        127–128
    site of, 44–46
    toasts at, 130–131
Registry, 94, 134–137

Rehearsal dinner, 103–115
Religious ceremony, 56–59
Religious conflicts, with wedding
        date, 44
Rings
    engagement, 16–23
    wedding, 125–126

Seating arrangements
    for reception, 127–128
    for rehearsal dinner, 113
Shoes, 77
Site
    of ceremony, 44–46
    of reception, 44–46
    of rehearsal dinner, 107–108
Socks, 77
Stress management, 159–162
Strip clubs, 150–151

Thank-you notes, 142–144
Ties, 74, 75
Time, of wedding, 42–44
Timeline
    for honeymoon planning, 86–88
    for wedding planning, 8–14
Toasts
    at reception, 130–131
    at rehearsal dinner, 113–115
Transportation, 118–124
Travel. See honeymoon
Travel agents, 98–99
Tuxedo, 71, 78–79

Venue. See site
Vows, writing of, 60–62

Waistcoats, 76
Wedding day, 156–159
Wedding insurance, 42
Wedding night, 88–89
Wedding party, 50–54
Wedding rings, 125–126
Wedding weekend, guest activities
        during, 115–116

Things to Do on Your Wedding Day

☐ Shave

☐ Get dressed, and have your best man or your parents look you over

☐ Put on your boutonniere

☐ Thank your parents for all they've done for you

☐ Give an envelope with the payment for the officiant and any other vendors to the best man or whomever you've designated to be the cash carrier

☐ If you've been holding onto your fiancée's wedding ring, hand it off to your best man–before the ceremony begins

☐ Smile for the camera during the formal photo session

☐ Look at your bride when you recite your vows

☐ Dance with your bride at the reception–more than once

☐ Eat–it sounds obvious, but many grooms skip this

☐ Schmooze with guests

☐ Cut the cake, and feed a piece to your new wife; don't shove it into her face

☐ Give a toast thanking your parents and guests–if you've chosen to do so

☐ Ride off into the sunset (or the wee hours of the morning) with your lovely bride

Things to Bring to the Wedding Site

- ☐ Jacket
- ☐ Pants
- ☐ Shirt
- ☐ Vest or cummerbund
- ☐ Tie or ascot
- ☐ Suspenders
- ☐ Cuff links and studs
- ☐ Shoes
- ☐ Socks
- ☐ Underwear
- ☐ Safety pins
- ☐ Lint brush

- ☐ Hairbrush and/or comb
- ☐ Hair gel or mousse
- ☐ Deodorant
- ☐ Breath freshener
- ☐ Headache medication
- ☐ Stomach soothing medication
- ☐ Extra pair of contact lenses
- ☐ Rewetting solution for contacts
- ☐ Toothbrush and toothpaste
- ☐ Dental floss

- ☐ Marriage license
- ☐ Bride's wedding ring, if you haven't already given it to your best man
- ☐ Copy of your vows, if you wrote your own
- ☐ Extra copies of readings or songs
- ☐ Any ceremonial objects you're providing
- ☐ Backup copy of the playlist for the band or DJ
- ☐ Notes for your toast, if applicable
- ☐ Payments for vendors
- ☐ Tips for vendors
- ☐ Clothing for exiting reception (if you're changing)
- ☐ Packed luggage for your wedding night (and honeymoon, if applicable)
- ☐ Honeymoon tickets, passports, driver's license, travel info, and other documents, if necessary
- ☐ Cell phone and charger
- ☐ Storage bag to hold any rented formalwear to be returned or formalwear you own so your best man or a family member can take it home for you

COUPON

Good for one
fifteen-minute
back rub

COUPON

Good for one night
out on the town
(with no wedding talk)

COUPON

Good for one weekend
of complete control
of the TV remote

COUPON

Good for one home-cooked
(or take-out) meal—
and I'll do the dishes